catawiki

Online
Chess auction

From the 13th through the 20th of November, Catawiki online auction house will host a special auction centred around chess.

✔ At this auction you will find rare **chess sets**, **books** and **curios**

✔ The auction starts at **12:00 o'clock** European time

✔ A **specialized auctioneer** guides the auction

www.catawiki.com/chess

Would you like to auction off your chess curios?

- High revenue
- Low commission fees
- International audience
- Secure sales

For more information: **www.catawiki.com/selling**

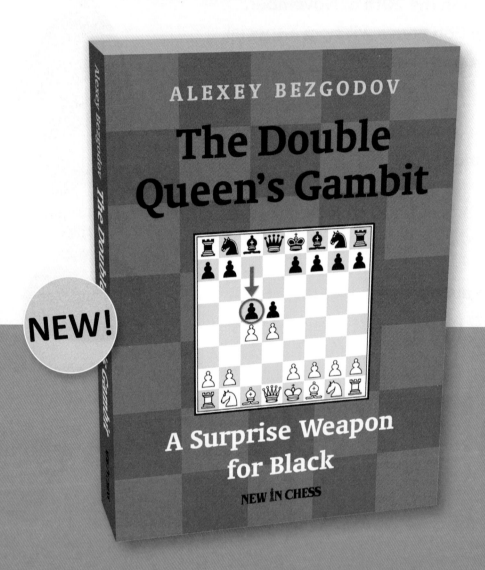

2015#7

NEW IN CHESS

Contents

'If by 2050 chess is still popular, we will all be champions.'

CONTRIBUTORS TO THIS ISSUE
Alina l'Ami, Levon Aronian, Jeroen Bosch, Pavel Eljanov, Anish Giri, Alexander Grischuk, Robert Hess, Dominic Lawson, Dylan McClain, Parimarjan Negi, Maxim Notkin, Arthur van de Oudeweetering, Judit Polgar, Hans Ree, Matthew Sadler, Nigel Short, Genna Sosonko, Jan Timman, Veselin Topalov, Loek van Wely

PHOTOS AND ILLUSTRATIONS
Phil Coomes (BBC), Maria Emelianova, David Llada, Lennart Ootes, Cathy Rogers, Berend Vonk

COVER
Levon Aronian: New In Chess

Wei Yi   Ding Liren

'It's nice when people are rooting for me. A guy like Garry Kasparov, one of my favourite players, probably my favourite player. I think he knows when he sees a good game.'
Levon Aronian

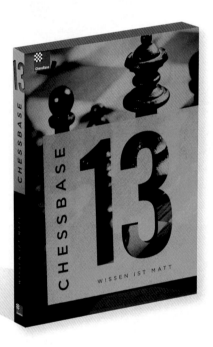

The best know best

Two years ago, I was privileged to be the host of the live commentary at the Alekhine Memorial, which moved from France to Russia halfway through It was an unforgettable experience. In Paris we stayed next–door to the Louvre, and in St. Petersburg in the imperial Grand Hotel Europe. But what I remember even more vividly were the broadcasts with Alexander Grischuk and Judit Polgar. They provided very knowledgeable comments, answered all my questions with consummate ease and treated the online audience to a wonderful chess show.

Both of them are present in this issue. With his dry humour, Alexander seeks for the objective truth of his win against Magnus Carlsen in the Sinquefield Cup. Judit delighted us by accepting our invitation to write a regular column.
As always, they show that the best players are also the best teachers, providing us with insights that make us enjoy chess and improve our game at the same time.

Don't miss Levon Aronian's sparkling game notes and revealing interview. Or Jan Timman's crystal–clear explanations. Or the inimitable Anish Giri, witty and original as ever, shedding his light on the World Cup in Baku, where he got as far as the semi–final.

Last time we surprised our subscribers with Anish's book *After Magnus* – a present, just because we wanted to thank you. And in fact we would like to thank you again, as your help in our recent promotion – send a free copy of New In Chess to a friend – was a resounding success and resulted in a considerable increase in our readership!
    This is our 30th anniversary issue. We believe that the best way to celebrate an anniversary is to continue doing what our readers have become attached to. Enjoying the games of the stars and the inspiring lessons and observations of our columnists.

The magazine you are holding is very different from what we started publishing 30 years ago: Bigger in size, full-colour, richer in content and now read by club players in 116 countries. But essentially nothing has changed. It's still about our passion for the very best in chess and our wish to share it.

Dirk Jan ten Geuzendam
Editor-in-Chief

'We believe that the best way to celebrate an anniversary is to continue doing what our readers have become attached to.'

Spectre of the past

ames Bond's eagerly awaited latest blockbuster, Spectre, goes on release in late October. And despite what the publicity shots might hint at, there's no much chess playing going on in this adventure with Daniel Craig, as the master spy tracks down his quarry to his Austrian bolthole, where across a conveniently placed chess set and board, he learns of the existence of Spectre.

The scene does, however, pay some homage to Bond's first encounter with Spectre from the original franchise — in *From Russia With Love* (starring Sean Connery) which featured a very famous chess scene. In it, we were introduced to Spectre's mastermind, as their tuxedo-clad top operative, Kronsteen (played superbly by Vladek Sheybal), is just about to administer the *coup de grâce* to win the Vienna International Chess Tournament.

For this scene, director Terence Young decided to adapt a brilliancy prize encounter from the 1960 USSR Championship, to wit the now equally famous King's Gambit duel between Boris Spassky and David Bronstein - the only difference being that in the 1963 Bond movie there were no White pawns on d4 and c5.

The reason for the omission remained a mystery for 40 years until it was revealed in a 2002 BBC Radio 4 documentary that the legendary Bond producers Albert 'Cubby' Broccoli and Harry Saltzman, mistakenly believed there to be a copyright on chess games, so they had the pawns removed from the board. A critical continuity error as it allowed a saving grace that wasn't available to Bronstein!

Because the Night

We've always had a fondness at the Café for 'punk's poet laureate' Patti Smith. But then, what's not to like about an artist who is able to simultaneously hold both the *Ordre des Arts et des Lettres* from the French ministry of culture and a place in the Rock and Roll Hall of Fame?

We were even more enamoured with the aging rocker (68) after hearing that Ms Smith's new book, *M Train* tells us more about her surreal

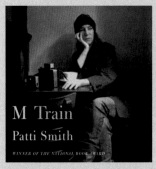

When Patti met Bobby.

midnight meeting with Bobby Fischer in August 2005, when the punk poet/singer was in Reykjavik on a European tour and asked to meet the reclusive former world champion.

Like Fischer, Smith was Chicago-born and New York-raised – and both went on to become icons from the same era. 'I had met him before', she recalled during an interview with the *New York Times*. 'When I was a young girl at Scribner's [a major New York bookshop] in the late '60s, I had the game department. He was supposed to do a book signing [*Bobby Fischer Teaches Chess*], and I stacked up all the books, and a lot of people came. He appeared very nervous, and he was only a couple of years older than me. He couldn't handle it, and I had to sneak him out the back door.'

In Reykjavik, when Smith reminded him of the bookshop meeting, he said, 'Can you still order books?' Being a lifelong bibliophile, Smith had retained a network of rare-book con-

tacts, and promised to help him out. 'If a book can be found, I can find it,' she said. And so for a time up to Fischer's death, she was his go-to for obscure history books.

During their new meeting, after some initial awkwardness between the two, she describes in the book how they suddenly found common ground again by singing the songs of Buddy Holly and others from the golden age of Rock'n Roll through until nearly dawn. 'Through the night we must have sung a hundred songs', recalls Smith. 'He knew every lyric to every fifties rock song, to every Motown song. He had all the dance moves.' At one point, she recalls, Fischer's bodyguard standing vigil outside the room burst in on the meeting, alarmed by hearing 'something strange.' It turned out to be the former world champion singing the falsetto chorus from 'Big Girls Don't Cry'.

The person Patti Smith mistakenly believed to be Fischer's 'bodyguard' was none other than the six-time Icelandic champion, GM Helgi Olafsson, who was the go-between to broker the meeting between the two, as he wrote in his book *Bobby Fischer Comes Home*.

The Lewis chesswoman

The Lewis chessmen are a fascinating mystery that continues to intrigue. Carved from walrus tusks in a style that points to the 12th century, found on a sandy beach in the Scottish Hebrides, and now divided between the British Museum and the National Museum of Scotland, they are rightly regarded as the world's most fabled and famous horde of chess-pieces.

But now in an intriguing new book, *Ivory Vikings: The Mystery of the Most Famous Chessmen in the World and the Woman Who Made Them*, American author and Norse authority, Nancy Marie Brown, claims to resolve the enigma of just who carved the pieces.

Using clues woven from medieval sagas, modern archaeology, art history

and what is known of Viking trade routes, Brown forensically examines theories placing the creation of these pieces firmly in Norway, Iceland or the northern island reaches of Scotland.

She also weighs evidence on who might have carved the ivory pieces,

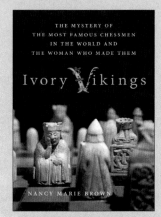

Was it really Margret the Adroit of Iceland?

'each face individual, each full of quirks: the king stout and stoic, the queen grieving or aghast, the bishops moon-faced and mild.' And the author favours the claim of a talented but obscure woman, Margret the Adroit of Iceland, whose reputed skill in ivory work and her patron's habit of sending gifts to the king of Norway and other notables are persuasive clues that she crafted the pieces.

The end of the lucky pen?

Remember the feeling of power you possessed by turning up to a tournament with a 'lucky' pen? Well, those halcyon days are set to end now, if the current trend is anything to go by. And not only pens, watches too – so you can forget about trying to imitate Garry Kasparov (with his ever-present Swiss marquee Audemars Piguet Royal Oak, the taking off and putting back on again during a game became something of a ritual) by also bringing along your expensive timepiece.

Cheating has got so rife now that during the World Cup in Baku players were banned from taking pens and wristwatches into the playing hall – and even our own contributing editor, Anish Giri, was somewhat peeved when he was told he couldn't wear his favourite bracelet. All of this left Hikaru Nakamura to tweet that these further restrictions were 'a sad day for chess.'

So why has it come to all this? FIDE explained that cheating technology has now gotten so sophisticated that tiny devices can be used to receive moves transmitted to players from their co-conspirators. Existing anti-cheating security measures – such as metal detectors before entering the tournament hall – are now not enough, say officials.

Pendants & Morse code

And we're betting that next on the FIDE hit list will now be pendants. Yes, that's right, pendants: the perfect finishing touch that once adorned the chest of any serious disco-going man from the 1970s. That's because, on the eve of the World Cup, Italian amateur Arcangelo Ricciardi was booted out of the Imperia Chess Festival in Liguria, Italy, when he was caught cheating with a suspected tiny video camera hidden in a pendant hanging from his neck.

Sending out an S.O.S.
Arcangelo Ricciardi

There were plenty of reasons to be suspicious of Ricciardi, such as the way he kept his thumb tucked into his armpit throughout several rounds, or his refusal to get up from his seat after hours of play. But you didn't need to be Sherlock Holmes to deduce that the deciding factor was probably that he had a rating of just 1868, yet was leaving grandmasters and international masters trailing in his wake.

But in the end, his eyes gave him away, according to arbiter Jean Coqueraut. The 37-year-old was 'batting his eyelids in the most unnatural way,' Coqueraut told the Italian newspaper *La Stampa*. 'Then I realised he was using Morse code.'

After refusing to remove his shirt when confronted, Ricciardi was sent through a metal detector. Hanging beneath his shirt, the detector found a pendant containing a tiny video camera connected to a small box underneath his armpit. It's believed Ricciardi was using the video camera to transmit his games to an accomplice, and then was being signalled back moves via Morse code to the armpit box, he was then picking up with his thumb.

Worryingly, the arbiter doubts whether winning the €1,000 first prize was his motive for the alleged cheating, and suspects that Ricciardi was perhaps road-testing the system for a titled player in a bigger tournament. On his part, Ricciardi naturally denied all the accusations, putting his newfound playing strength down to yoga and self-training, further adding that the suspicious pendant was merely just his 'good-luck charm'.

Bad Guinness

Since 2004, Edward Winter, that purveyor of all things history and truth, has kept a 'keen' eye on the chess content in the Guinness World Records. So good at the job is he, that a certain English chess journalist even managed to set his own personal plagiarism record by shamelessly lifting verbatim several detailed paragraphs by Winter for a column in his own name.

Reporting on the ever-dwindling chess content in *Guinness World Records*, Winter wrote of the 2010 edition that 'the combined items receive considerably less space than, for instance, the illustrated feature on page 161 regarding a German who, in two minutes, "removed 26 garter belts from the legs of willing volunteers using just his teeth"'. He would therefore have been overjoyed to read the FIDE missive on a 'successful' visit made by Kirsan Ilyumzhinov to the editorial offices in London of the Guinness World Records, as he dropped in en passant to offer his congratulations from the chess fraternity on their 60th anniversary.

The missive showed a beaming photo of the FIDE president with Craig

For the record: FIDE President Kirsan Ilyumzhinov and Craig Glenday with the 2015 edition of Guinness World Records.

Glenday, the Editor-in-Chief, proudly holding between them the 2015 edition of the book. We were told that FIDE had had positive talks about cooperation with the Records' representatives on future chess content and were looking at how best to present them in the book.

So with that in mind, we looked forward to the arrival of the 2016 *Guinness World Records*. And when it did finally land on our doorstep, we frantically flicked through the pages to discover the number of chess-related items in the 2016 edition to be: zero, zip, zilch and nada! ∎

Herman Steiner's Hollywood

Re Bruce Monson's article on Herman Steiner in New In Chess 2015/6. In *American Chess Bulletin*, January 1933 Vol. 30(1) page 15, a brief item states that 'Herman Steiner, who remains in California after playing in the Pasadena Tournament, played simultanously at 78 boards (teams and individuals), at the Los Angeles Athletic Club on January 7. The young New Yorker made a truly splendid score which comprised 69 wins, 3 draws and 6 losses.'

Dr. Bernard Christenson
Guaynabo, Puerto Rico

The lost French manuscript

I was pleased to read in New In Chess 2015/5 that the Franco-English GM Matthew Sadler had discovered, or rediscovered, one of the best games commentators ever in the person of Savielly Tartakower. As a former chess journalist and former chess editor at the publishing house Éditions Payot-Rivages, I would like to add a few comments for your readers concerning a mystery involving the great champion and one of his French manuscripts. But to begin with we should thank Russell Enterprises for making available to an English audience the sparkling prose of a unique player. Technically speaking, the reissued manuscript is still within the framework of the translation by Harry Golombek, who sometimes had great trouble to transfer into English the sparkling and brilliant liberties that Tartakower allowed himself with the French grammar.

Apart from prizes that he won in tournaments – immediately 'sacrificed' in the nearest casino (Tartakower was an inveterate gambler) – 'Tarta', as he was called in Parisian circles, annotated many games for chess magazines all over Europe, translating them himself. Thus, for the same work, the revenues were multiplied. Alekhine worked in the same manner, thanks to carbon paper, which required additional accuracy, variations were double- or triplechecked. The result of the collaboration of these two men was *200 Parties d'Echecs* (200 Games of Chess), which was published under Alekhine's name, reworked for the French edition by Tarta... and finally published in English by *British Chess Magazine*, with Alekhine donating the proceeds of this

Write to us
New In Chess, P.O. Box 1093
1810 KB Alkmaar, The Netherlands
or e-mail: editors@newinchess.com
Letters may be edited or abridged

manuscript to the French Federation.

After this preamble I'd like to draw your attention to the aforesaid mystery: *Tartakower's My best games of chess 1905-1954* is what the one-volume edition is called in English. The translation has not been changed in more than 60 years; it is still Golombek's. In France, the plan was to have the same manuscript published in two volumes. The first volume appeared with Stock in 1953 with the iconoclastic French title: *Tartacover vous parle* (Tartakower speaks to you). The second edition was published by Payot in 1992, followed by several pocket-book editions with different covers. The annotated games stop in 1931.

What has happened to the second manuscript of the annotated games (from 1931 to 1954) that the Master had necessarily passed on to the translator? A mystery. When Tartakower suddenly died on February 4, 1956, the young Claude Lemoine (b. 1932 – and future champion of France – in 1958), went to his hotel room, where, as he told me, 'There was nothing. No papers, no books. Tartakower lived in abject poverty.'

I had the good fortune to meet arbiter Golombek (1911-1995) for the first time at the Hastings tournament in 1980. He had summoned me and the young Manuel Apicella (now a GM) to reprimand us for fixing a draw, as we had replayed Sam Loyd's famous double stalemate in 12 moves with all pieces on the board.

In late 1994, I tried to phone him to see if he had retained the second part of the French manuscript, but I was told he had just had a stroke.

In France, it was suggested to me to do research in the Military Archives. But although Tartakower served his adopted country (he was a member of the Resistance during World War II), I have strong doubts about his organizational skills and find it even harder to believe that he would entrust any document to a military institution!

It is quite frustrating to read an English translation (of the post 1931 games) from a sparkling French which can no longer be reconstructed and that you can only guess about. In both volumes the mischievous mind of that devilish Tarta can sometimes be felt in a turn of phrase or a variation. That is when Tartakower speaks to us. And Tartakower is still speaking to us, regardless the language in which he comes to us, and that is what matters.

Christophe Bouton
Saint Germain en Laye, France

COLOPHON

PUBLISHER: Allard Hoogland
EDITORS-IN-CHIEF:
Dirk Jan ten Geuzendam, Jan Timman
CONTRIBUTING EDITOR: Anish Giri
EDITORS: Peter Boel, René Olthof
ART-DIRECTION: Jan Scholtus
PRODUCTION: Joop de Groot
TRANSLATORS:
Sarah Hurst, Ken Neat, Piet Verhagen
SALES AND ADVERTISING: Remmelt Otten

Q No part of this magazine may be reproduced, stored in a retrieval system or transmitted in any form or by any means, recording or otherwise, without the prior permission of the publisher.

**NEW IN CHESS
P.O. BOX 1093
1810 KB ALKMAAR
THE NETHERLANDS**

PHONE: 00-31-(0)72-51 27 137
FAX: 00-31-(0)72-51 58 234
E-MAIL:
SUBSCRIPTIONS: nic@newinchess.com
EDITORS: editors@newinchess.com
SALES AND ADVERTISING:
otten@newinchess.com

BANK DETAILS:
IBAN: NL41ABNA 0589126024
BIC: ABNANL2A in favour of Interchess BV,
Alkmaar, The Netherlands

WWW.NEWINCHESS.COM

Top seeds rarely do well in knockout tournaments

In September, Magnus Carlsen, the reigning World Champion, proposed changing the system by which the World Championship is decided from a series of qualifying events, leading up to a match, to an annual knockout tournament, like the World Cup. Carlsen said that a knockout tournament would do away with the traditional advantage that the champion has and also give more players a chance to win the title. Indeed, if history is any guide, that is true. As the graphic below shows, the top seeds have trouble even making it to the quarterfinals and the top seed has only won twice, while a top-five seed has won only half the time.

DYLAN LOEB McCLAIN

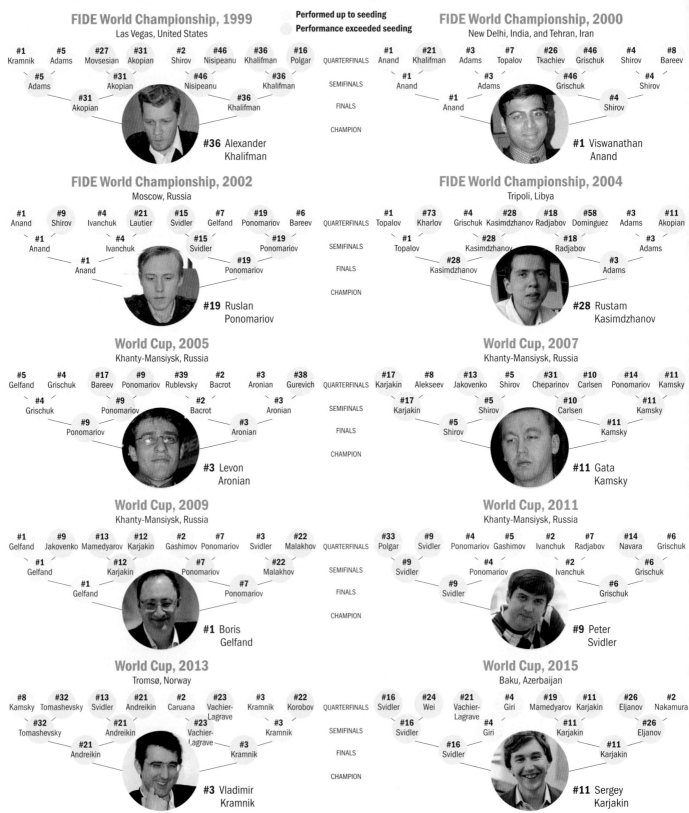

Performed up to seeding
Performance exceeded seeding

FIDE World Championship, 1999
Las Vegas, United States
#1 Kramnik, #5 Adams, #27 Movsesian, #31 Akopian, #2 Shirov, #46 Nisipeanu, #36 Khalifman, #16 Polgar
#5 Adams, #31 Akopian, #46 Nisipeanu, #36 Khalifman
#31 Akopian, #36 Khalifman
#36 Alexander Khalifman

FIDE World Championship, 2000
New Delhi, India, and Tehran, Iran
#1 Anand, #21 Khalifman, #3 Adams, #7 Topalov, #26 Tkachiev, #46 Grischuk, #4 Shirov, #8 Bareev
#1 Anand, #3 Adams, #46 Grischuk, #4 Shirov
#1 Anand, #4 Shirov
#1 Viswanathan Anand

FIDE World Championship, 2002
Moscow, Russia
#1 Anand, #9 Shirov, #4 Ivanchuk, #21 Lautier, #15 Svidler, #7 Gelfand, #19 Ponomariov, #6 Bareev
#1 Anand, #4 Ivanchuk, #15 Svidler, #19 Ponomariov
#1 Anand, #19 Ponomariov
#19 Ruslan Ponomariov

FIDE World Championship, 2004
Tripoli, Libya
#1 Topalov, #73 Kharlov, #4 Grischuk, #28 Kasimdzhanov, #18 Radjabov, #58 Dominguez, #3 Adams, #11 Akopian
#1 Topalov, #28 Kasimdzhanov, #18 Radjabov, #3 Adams
#28 Kasimdzhanov, #3 Adams
#28 Rustam Kasimdzhanov

World Cup, 2005
Khanty-Mansiysk, Russia
#5 Gelfand, #4 Grischuk, #17 Bareev, #9 Ponomariov, #39 Rublevsky, #2 Bacrot, #3 Aronian, #38 Gurevich
#4 Grischuk, #9 Ponomariov, #2 Bacrot, #3 Aronian
#9 Ponomariov, #3 Aronian
#3 Levon Aronian

World Cup, 2007
Khanty-Mansiysk, Russia
#17 Karjakin, #8 Alekseev, #13 Jakovenko, #5 Shirov, #31 Cheparinov, #10 Carlsen, #14 Ponomariov, #11 Kamsky
#17 Karjakin, #5 Shirov, #10 Carlsen, #11 Kamsky
#5 Shirov, #11 Kamsky
#11 Gata Kamsky

World Cup, 2009
Khanty-Mansiysk, Russia
#1 Gelfand, #9 Jakovenko, #13 Mamedyarov, #12 Karjakin, #2 Gashimov, #7 Ponomariov, #3 Svidler, #22 Malakhov
#1 Gelfand, #12 Karjakin, #7 Ponomariov, #22 Malakhov
#1 Gelfand, #7 Ponomariov
#1 Boris Gelfand

World Cup, 2011
Khanty-Mansiysk, Russia
#33 Polgar, #9 Svidler, #4 Ponomariov, #5 Gashimov, #2 Ivanchuk, #7 Radjabov, #14 Navara, #6 Grischuk
#9 Svidler, #4 Ponomariov, #2 Ivanchuk, #6 Grischuk
#9 Svidler, #6 Grischuk
#9 Peter Svidler

World Cup, 2013
Tromsø, Norway
#8 Kamsky, #32 Tomashevsky, #13 Svidler, #21 Andreikin, #2 Caruana, #23 Vachier-Lagrave, #3 Kramnik, #22 Korobov
#32 Tomashevsky, #21 Andreikin, #23 Vachier-Lagrave, #3 Kramnik
#21 Andreikin, #3 Kramnik
#3 Vladimir Kramnik

World Cup, 2015
Baku, Azerbaijan
#16 Svidler, #24 Wei, #21 Vachier-Lagrave, #4 Giri, #19 Mamedyarov, #11 Karjakin, #26 Eljanov, #2 Nakamura
#16 Svidler, #4 Giri, #11 Karjakin, #26 Eljanov
#16 Svidler, #11 Karjakin
#11 Sergey Karjakin

QUARTERFINALS · SEMIFINALS · FINALS · CHAMPION

Pal Benko: 'In the Soviets' view, chess was not merely an art or a science or even a sport; it was what it had been invented to simulate: war.'

David Hockney: 'Drawing is rather like playing chess: your mind races ahead of the moves that you eventually make.'

Rodney Martin: 'The tensions have been high between the two Koreas, but we have to understand that South Korea is an artificially created country, artificially created by the United States to be a chess piece in its Cold War battle with the former Soviet Union.'
(The former US congressional staffer-turned political analyst and radio host)

J.H. Blackburne: 'I find that whisky is a most useful stimulus to mental activity, especially when one is engaged in a stiff and prolonged struggle. All chess masters indulge moderately in wines or spirits. Speaking for myself, alcohol clears my brain and I always take a glass or two when playing.'
(The English master interviewed by the anti-temperance journal, Licensing World)

Garry Kasparov: 'Could be worse. My main worry is if the film promotes chess or not.'
(When asked after attending a screening in St. Louis of Pawn Sacrifice, on whether or not he liked the movie.)

Lord Rosebery: 'At chess he [Napoleon] was eminently unskilled and it taxed all the courtliness of his suite to avoid defeating him: a simple trickery which he sometimes perceived.'
(from: Napoleon: the Last Phase - London, 1900)

Maarten 't Hart: 'Why am I such a useless chess player? Why do I have the lowest Elo-rating in the world? Why has studying theory books never made the slightest bit of difference to my play? Why can anyone who knows the game beat me hands down? I always lose against my computer even if I put it at its lowest possible level. And the strange thing is: when I learned to play chess, I found it such a wonderful game. And I still find it a wonderful game.'
(The Dutch novelist in the book of the 1996 VSB tournament in Amsterdam)

Gerrit Krol: 'Why, oh why am I not a good chess player? I really think I should be; it fits me so well. I am not particularly fond of games, or playing – but I like chess. If for whatever reason I was forced to play chess for two hours every day, I would not mind. I have been playing chess since I was six – and I am still no good at it.'
(Another Dutch writer who doesn't get it)

Pierre van Hooijdonk: 'The important thing is that you know what you want and understand the moves going on behind the scenes and inside clubs. If you can read that, it's like a game of chess. You need to know, this is happening here and that is happening there.'
(The Dutch soccer star on the transfer saga involving his countryman, Robin van Persie, before his summer move from Manchester United to Fenerbahçe)

Magnus Carlsen: 'I am not only a chess player, I am a chess fan and a chess nerd. I want to follow everything that happens.'
(Being distracted during a major interview with The Financial Times, as he followed the World Cup in Baku on his phone)

Jennifer Shahade: 'Playing chess is more athletic than artistic. Champions are more concerned with victory than beauty: it's war with occasionally graceful kicks.'

Jonathan Hawkins: 'Please don't fall into the trap of convincing yourself that once you organise your openings completely, then you will move onto other areas of study. That day will never come; at least it still hasn't for me. In terms of memorising variations, especially for players rated 2000 or under, I would tone this down to approximately 10% of your study time or less.'
(The proven road to success for the new double British champion, in his book From Amateur to IM: Proven Ideas and Training Methods)

Ron Livingston: 'Life is not always like chess. Just because you have the king surrounded, don't think he is not capable of hurting you.'
(The American actor who starred in Office Space and Band of Brothers)

Lars von Trier: 'Far be it from me to force anyone into either chess or dressage, but if you choose to do so yourself, in my opinion there is only one way: follow the rules.'

Karjakin prevails in mind-boggling marathon

Their fervent wish had been to reach the final of the World Cup and thus qualify for the Candidates' tournament. Once this mission was accomplished, Sergey Karjakin and Peter Svidler, the last two men standing in Baku, had a bonus to play for: first prize was $120,000, while the runner-up would get $80,000. In a 10-game slugfest riddled with blunders and without a single draw, the young Russian brought home the bacon. Semi-finalist **ANISH GIRI** reports.

T The World Cup, not to be confused with the World Championship (no longer and not yet!) is one of the rare knock-out events on the elite chess circuit. One hundred and twenty-eight players battle for only two coveted spots in the Candidates' Tournament, meaning that in order to get there one has to overcome six strong opponents in two-game mini-matches, followed by a tiebreak on the next day if needed. The two lucky players that reach the final play another four games (plus tiebreak if necessary) to determine

As Sergey Karjakin lifts the World Cup trophy, runner-up Peter Svidler manages a smile concealing the disgust and disbelief he must feel after all the chances he missed.

the World Cup winner. The winner takes home $120,000, the runner-up $80,000. Lasting close to four weeks, the World Cup is essentially a real-life demonstration of the survival of the fittest, with the quality of the games gradually receding into the background, while character and nerves move to the fore.

FIDE offers this event as a package together with the Chess Olympiad. If you want to host the Olympiad, you also have to organize the World Cup in the preceding year. Next year the Olympiad will be held in Baku, so for the 2015 World Cup 128, of us (yes, I was there too) were treated to a luxury stay at the Fairmont Hotel in the iconic Flame Towers complex high above the bay of Baku. The estimated building cost of the Flame Towers was $350 million and the hotel in the North Tower is a work of art, with interior details that definitely made me jealous, coming from my newly acquired apartment. Think three-metre tall glass windows and built-in TV in the bathroom mirror.

On top of that, the organization

> ‘Lasting close to four weeks, the World Cup is essentially a real-life demonstration of the survival of the fittest.’

was excellent and the little detail that the usual 20-percent FIDE tax on the prize-money was going to be taken care of by the organizers was a comforting thought and some consolation for the players that sadly got knocked out.

It's impossible to cover 128 players and a pretty insane number of brilliant (and not so brilliant) games, so in order to leave some space for other great contributors (no Nigel S. jokes this time) I have decided to discuss the tournament of a few players, and try to get into the heads of the winners and the losers.

These are my heroes. The Losers: Levon Aronian, Vladimir Kramnik. The Winners: Peter Svidler, Sergey Karjakin. The Pavel Eljanov: Pavel Eljanov.

Levon Aronian

Lev was probably ecstatic after his victory in the Sinquefield Cup (Am I back??!!), but the rules of the World Cup are quite different. Although he looked pretty comfortable playing in Baku, he got knocked out as early as Round 2. I had the idea that he wasn't putting too much pressure on himself, but this was probably his last chance (not counting a possible wild card) to get into the Candidates'. To say that it was a surprise when Levon got knocked out by Areshchenko (great player, but still...) is to say nothing. Missing an advantage in the second classical game was bad news for the Armenian hero, but the decisive blow came in the first rapid game, when he spoiled a dangerous initiative and blundered in the endgame.

And the problem with getting knocked out in the World Cup is that it's over and bye-bye, time to go home. The fact that Levon proposed a double knock-out system after the tournament was endearing, but sometimes you only get one shot, one chance.

Vladimir Kramnik

Big Vlad came to Baku with big ambitions – a month of hard work behind him (no reason not to believe him on this one) and sporting stylish sunglasses that seemed like a big statement. He had an impressive start, with lots of variations in the post-game interviews. That's the great Kramnik we know, but his tournament ended rather abruptly as well. He had only himself to blame, though. Not winning the following

Vladimir Kramnik came to Baku with big ambitions, but in Round 3 he was abruptly eliminated by Dmitry Andreikin, the opponent he defeated two years ago in the final of the Tromsø World Cup.

BAKU

game against Dmitry Andreikin was enough to get knocked out.

Kramnik-Andreikin
Baku 2015 (3.3)
position after 30.♘d4

So far the game had been quite complicated and although at times it seemed like Andreikin was under pressure, he handled the middlegame pretty well. Now he is about to finally free his rook from a7. First, though, he has to take care of the other rook.
30...♖d6?? Any move without blundering a fork would be fine. Pick a square: e8, e6 or e4. **31.♘c8** Of course. In fact Dmitry blundered two forks, as White could have also gone 31.♘d5 followed by ♘b5. **31...♖a8 32.♘xd6 ♗xd6**

Black is dead lost, but Kramnik managed to complicate his task and in the end had to settle for a draw.

More big names fell by the wayside: Caruana (who lost to Mamedyarov), Topalov (to Svidler), Nakamura (reached the quarterfinal, but then lost to Eljanov, a separate chapter in this article) and many more favourites.

Me

I was the last top-10 player to leave the stage. After having had trouble dealing with Arthur Ssegwanyi from Uganda, I managed to recover, winning the tiebreak against Alexander Motylev 2-0 (later on I would also win the tiebreak against Radek Wojtaszek 2-0). One of my highlights was a nice endgame victory against Peter Leko.

NOTES BY
Anish Giri

CA 5.12 – E05
Anish Giri
Peter Leko
Baku 2015 (3.2)

I would have talked a lot about the importance of the white game in a two-game match, had I not lost in the semi-finals against Peter Svidler precisely due to my refusal to abandon the idea of the advantage of the white pieces, when I should have contented myself with a draw in my white game...
1.d4 ♘f6 2.c4 e6 3.g3
I have had many memorable moments connected with the Catalan. While the opening is considered to be pretty dull and harmless, I have managed to win and lose quite a bunch of games with it.
3...d5 4.♗g2 ♗e7 5.♘f3 0-0 6.0-0 dxc4 7.♕c2 a6 8.a4

I have also taken the pawn at once, but this move, stopping ...b5, has been quite fashionable lately.

8...♗d7 9.♕xc4 ♗c6 10.♗g5
A small surprise, as previously I have only played 10.♗f4, which is just as critical.

10...♗d5
The latest trend, returning to the roots. For a while it was thought that Black doesn't need the early ...c5 break, but after some games involving some booked-up people, it turned out to be less easy than it seemed.
10...h6 is what I have done myself twice in the 'Youth' vs. 'Experience' tournament in Amsterdam, back in the day when I was still considered to be 'Youth': 11.♗xf6 ♗xf6 12.♘c3 ♗xf3 13.♗xf3 c6 14.♕b3 ♖a7, and here I held my own after 15.a5, but not after 15.♘e4!?.
11.♕c2 ♗e4

12.♕d1
This is a pretty big line, with the most recent game having been won by Hikaru Nakamura against Vishy Anand. Curiously enough, and not inspired by that game or the one we're talking about now, Eljanov later went on to beat Hikaru after 12.♕c1!?, stopping ...c5 altogether (see Pavel's notes to that game in this report).

Needless to say, that's a 'pretty big' line too.

12...c5 13.dxc5 ♗xc5

14.♘bd2 Hikaru played 14.♕xd8 ♖xd8 15.♘bd2 ♗c6 16.♘b3 ♗e7 17.♘a5, and here, too, Black had to answer some unpleasant questions. I believed, however, that Peter Leko would have already figured out how to answer those.

14...♗c6 15.♘e5 ♗xg2 16.♔xg2 This position is not new either. It doesn't look like anything at all for White. Black has successfully neutralized the famous Catalan bishop and seems to have no weaknesses. However, after studying this type of position deeply, I realized that the established system of coordinates needs to be reassessed.

16...♗e7
A new move, but as it is so natural it obviously didn't escape my attention. 16...♘bd7 allows 17.♘xd7 ♕xd7 18.♗xf6 gxf6, which is probably why Peter played 16...♗e7 first. This structure with knight vs. bishop is quite common in the Catalan and I believe it was Ulf Andersson (the name Zoltan Ribli comes to mind as

The 2015 World Cup was held in the spectacular Fairmont Baku Hotel in the north tower of the iconic Flame Towers.

well!) who was squeezing them out, back in the days.

Nowadays, the squeezing mechanisms have changed somewhat, but the squeezing itself remains, as I have managed to show in this game, as well as in my game against Veselin Topalov from Stavanger. 16...♘d4 17.♘df3 ♗xb2 18.♖b1 ♗e5 19.♘xe5 was seen in Li Chao-Xiu Deshun, two years ago. The mighty Li Chao managed to win this game, though I have always believed that after 19...b5!?, with pawns only on the right wing, Black should be able to hold this position.

17.♖c1 ♘bd7

18.♘xd7!? I was hoping for this to be a surprise for Peter. This and the following move look incredibly harmless, but the position contains some hidden venom.

18.♘dc4 looks far more natural, but after 18...♘xe5 19.♘xe5 ♕a5 20.♗xf6 ♗xf6 21.♘d7 ♖fd8 22.♘xf6+ gxf6 the pressure is gone, as the doubled f-pawns are hardly a nuisance with only major pieces on the board.

18...♕xd7 19.♘f3

19...♕xd1 The alternative is 19...♖fd8, but then White might keep the queens on with 20.♕b3, although it is questionable whether the rook on d7 is so well placed after 20.♕xd7 ♖xd7. White controls the c-file after 21.♖c2, followed by ♖fc1.

20.♖fxd1 ♖fc8
Now you would think that ...♔f8-e8 will follow, with a quick handshake. However, the white knight has some jumping potential, and a white pawn expansion on the kingside is something for Black to worry about as well in the near future.

21.♞e5

21...h6

21...♔f8!? first makes sense as well, so that White is unable to go f4 without shutting out his bishop outside the pawn chain. Still, after 22.f4!? ♔e8 23.♔f3 h6 24.♗h4!? White retains unpleasant pressure. Black is unable to untangle himself and has run out of moves already, while White has only started.

22.♗d2

22...♖d8

Played after a very long think. Usually such moves, especially after a long think, are quite bad, but this is one of the rare exceptions. In fact, the idea is quite clever, but I wasn't planning to give up hope.

22...♔f8 is more natural. Here Peter was afraid of the unpleasant 23.f4 (I was thinking of 23.♞c4!?, planning to follow up with the simple 24.f4 and 25.♔f3, advancing a little bit) 23...♔e8 24.♔f3 ♖xc1 (24...♞d7? 25.♖xc8+ ♖xc8 26.♞xd7 ♔xd7 27.♗c3+ is an important idea that stops Black from simplifying) 25.♖xc1 ♞d7 26.♞d3 ♔d8.

ANALYSIS DIAGRAM

This is the plan that Peter was trying later, but it doesn't solve the problems. Black is one move too slow: 27.♗a5+!? b6 28.♗c3 f6 29.a5! b5 30.♗b4!, with some bad news.

'Now I started making some sophisticated moves. I don't know about their real value, but Peter was definitely not pleased.'

23.♞d3!? A big positional mistake would be 23.♗a5?: 23...♖xd1! 24.♖xd1 ♖c8!. It's all about the c-file here, as the d7-square is safely guarded. Here it is time for a handshake indeed.

23...♖dc8 Now I just proceed with my plan, although the fact that Black

got the option of ...♞d7 was indeed worth two tempi.

23...♖ac8 is not much better: 24.♗a5! ♖e8 25.f4, with the same pressure.

24.f4

24...♔f8

Going for a passive approach. This backfired in the game, though up to some point it seemed justified.

24...♞e4!? 25.♗e3 f5 doesn't solve the problems, but at least Black has a nice knight.

25.♔f3 ♞d7 Now I started making some sophisticated moves. I don't know about their real value, but Peter was definitely not pleased.

26.♗e3

26.e4 ♞c5 was an option I would rather avoid, although there are some issues here as well for Black: 27.♞xc5 ♖xc5 28.♗e3 ♖xc1 29.♖xc1 ♗d8, and Black is far from solving his problems. Once he will be ready to exchange rooks, there will be some problems on the kingside: 30.h4 ♔e8 31.h5 ♔d7 32.g4 ♖c8 33.♖xc8 ♔xc8 34.♗d4 f6 35.♗c5, and White wins.

26...♔e8 27.♗d4!

It's always useful to ask questions.

Here Black stands before a very painful junction.

27...♗f6

27...g6 leaves the kingside quite vulnerable. After 28.g4 ♖xc1 29.♖xc1 ♔d8 30.♗g7 h5 31.gxh5 gxh5 White can switch: 32.♗c3 ♖c8 33.♖g1!.

The move I had expected was 27...f6, but here, too, the problems are unsolvable: 28.e4 ♖xc1 29.♖xc1 ♔d8 30.♔g4!? g6 31.f5. Black should probably abandon the idea of exchanging the rooks, but then it is quite hard to play without any clear plan.

28.♗xf6!

Correctly judging that even without the bishops, or perhaps especially without the bishops, White actually gets something real.

28...♘xf6

28...gxf6 is not a move you make easily. Here even the brutal ♔g4-h5 comes to mind. Remember that pawn ending you studied as a child?

29.♘e5! ♔e7

With the idea of ...♘e8. Here I felt some vibes of relief from Peter, but I knew they wouldn't last too long.

30.e4 ♖xc1 31.♖xc1

31...♘e8 This is a very nice and solid plan, covering the c7-square. It would seem that there is no way for White to improve his pieces. Also, Black has the idea of actually going ...♘d6, preparing ...♖c8, as the check on c7 is rather harmless.

Therefore it is about time for the white knight to be rerouted.

32.♘d3! a5

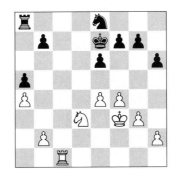

Once again a clever defensive attempt. The problem was that even if Black would be able to exchange rooks, ♘c5 would still often win White a pawn. Now, though, a whole new bunch of weak squares has been created on the queenside.

33.♖c5!?

33...♔d6?

Finally, Peter cracks under time-pressure. This move looks awful and was played in an impulse.

He should have played 33...♖d8! 34.♔e3 b6, in the style of the preceding defence. Black would attain a decent defensive set-up with the rook on d6 if needed, but it's clear that the misery has only just started. The b6-pawn is weak, as is the c6-square. The next step for White is to advance his kingside pawns, fishing for more weaknesses.

34.♖c3!

It's possible to miss this move, but once it has been made, it is clear that Black is in trouble. There are too many threats now, as e5+ is an idea as well.

34...♖a6 Maybe the best defence was 34...f6, as now the position becomes ready for a concrete solution. 34...♔e7 is met by 35.♖b3! and 34...♖b8 by 35.♘e5!.

35.e5+!

35...♔e7 36.♘c5 Not the only way, but the most brutal one.

36...♖b6 37.♘d3! ♖xb2 38.♖d7+ ♔f8 39.♘xb7! Now not only is the a5-pawn hanging, there is also the idea of ♘d8, which, as it will turn out, was what Peter had missed.

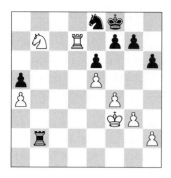

39...♖b3+ 39...♖c2 defends against 40.♘d8, but now I pick up the pawn: 40.♘xa5 ♖xh2 (40...♖a2 41.♘b7! ♖xa4 42.♘d8) 41.♘b7! ♖c2 42.a5, and with the passer the win is a matter of simple technique.
40.♔g4

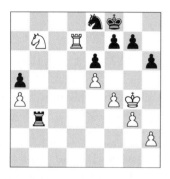

40...♖b4 Missing the main idea, but the position was already lost anyhow. 40...g6 was the only chance, with the idea of meeting 41.♘d8 with 41... f5+!, followed by ...♘g7. But here the cleanest way is the nice 41.♘xa5 ♖b4 42.♘c6 ♖xa4 43.♘d8 f5+ 44.♔h3 ♘g7 45.♘f7!, and even with all pawns on the same side, Black is absolutely lost.

41.♘d8!
This was far too enjoyable. Not only is the black knight totally dominated, the whole kingside is collapsing as well. The rest was unnecessary.

41...♔g8 42.♖e7 f5+ 43.♔h5 ♔h7 44.♖xe8 ♖b2 Forcing a couple of only moves, but not the hardest ones.

45.h3 ♖h2 46.♔h4
Black resigned.

In Round 5, I managed to beat the very strong knock-out fighter MVL. I won a pawn with White against the Grünfeld and after a long fight I eventually managed to convert it in a study-like rook ending.

In the semi-final I was paired up with Peter Svidler, who had just managed to beat Wei Yi. I must be honest: after I had seen how many chances Svidler had left unused in his match against Wei Yi, I lost all sense of danger.

NOTES BY
Anish Giri

RL 26.8 – C92
Anish Giri
Peter Svidler
Baku 2015 (6.1)

1.e4
During my preparation I was somewhat disappointed that our match was so short. It would have been nice to ask Peter some more questions.
1...e5 2.♘f3 ♘c6 3.♗b5 a6
Lately, Peter has been opting for the Ruy Lopez, although the Sicilian was also in his repertoire until just very recently.
4.♗a4 ♘f6 5.0-0 ♗e7 6.♖e1 b5 7.♗b3 0-0 8.c3 d6 9.h3 ♗b7 10.d4 ♖e8 11.♘bd2 exd4 12.cxd4 ♘d7
One of the systems that Peter employs in the Spanish. A certain chess lover wrote an article about it in a certain chess publication and claimed to have shared his analysis on this topic with a certain 2700+ player. Seeing Peter playing it four times in a row gave us a good hint of who that 2700+ player might be.

13.♘f1 ♞a5 14.♗c2 ♗f6 15.♖b1

Not a very critical move. Now Black gets a version of the Benoni structure.

15...c5 16.d5 ♞c4 The knight has to join the game, as 17.b3 was already a major positional threat.

17.b3 ♞ce5 18.♘3h2

Keeping more pieces on the board. I was reasonably happy with my position; my next few moves are clear.

18...♞g6 19.♘g3 ♗c8

Logical. Having the bishop on b7 makes little sense in the Benoni.

20.♖f1!?

Trying to be too clever. 20.♘g4 ♗c3 was bothering me a little bit.

20...♞b6 21.♘g4 I had many options and I am no longer certain this move is as good as it seemed then.

Peter Svidler is meticulously searched before the game. The anti-cheating measures were very strict. The players were not even allowed to wear watches or bring their own pen.

21...♗xg4!

22.hxg4 At this point, I already started having some doubts about my future in this game. The kingside attack is easy to set up, but the mate will be exceptionally hard to deliver. In view of that, taking with the queen deserved attention as well.

22...h6 23.♘f5

Once again, not sure.

23...♞e7

24.♘e3

24.g3 looks very logical, followed by a quick ♔g2 and ♖h1. Then, at some point Black will stop the threat of ♗xh6 with either ...♗g5 or even ... ♔f8, and it will not be so clear who will be first, as White's plan of g4-g5 is not that dangerous, while the advance of the a6-pawn, though not dangerous either, is somewhat bothering.

24...b4

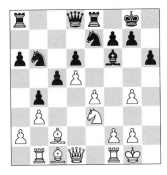

25.g3

Again I had different options. 25.a4 was interesting, but I felt very bad about distracting my bishop from c1, where it is staring at the h6-pawn. In fact, from here on in, I was calculating the positions, as Black basically is going to play ...a5, ...a4, ...axb3, ...♖a3, no matter what. I didn't see how my attack was going to succeed, but I thought that I should just make those moves until something came up. But nothing came up. ☺

25...a5

26.♔g2

Once again, 26.a4 was a good idea, but 26...bxa3 27.♗xa3 didn't look too threatening. Still, here White is really unlikely to ever end up worse, while in the game there were no longer any guarantees.

26...a4 27.bxa4

Here I thought I would bail out, but the hesitation was still there.

27...♕d7

28.♕d3?

Played after a very long think and almost with the realization that this was not the way to go. I should have played 28.a3! ♘xa4 29.♗xa4 ♖xa4 30.axb4 (30.♘c4 was my original intention when I played 27.bxa4, but then I noticed 30...bxa3!) 30...♖xb4 31.♖xb4 cxb4, and here White has a pretty silly position, with no hope of an initiative. On the other hand, a few more moves and the game will peter out. This sounded like a bad thing to me at this point, but one move later I deeply regretted what I had done.

28...♘g6

29.♘f5?

The last way out was 29.a3!, but the further you go in the mud the deeper you sink.

29...♘xa4 30.♗xa4

Here I offered a draw, hoping Peter might not yet realize how absurd my play was and also having in mind how many draws he had taken in winning positions in this World Cup. But a player like Peter always smells blood.

30...♖xa4 31.♖h1 ♘e7

The most precise. Now White has no ideas on the kingside and his bridges have already been burnt. The rest is agony.

32.g5 hxg5 33.♘e3 ♖xa2 34.♗d2 ♘g6 35.♘f5 ♘e5 36.♕e2 g6

37.♘h6+ After the game Peter pretended that he had missed 37.♗xg5, but I am almost certain he just wanted to look cool after 37...♖xe2 38.♗xf6 ♖xf2+ 39.♔g1 ♖h2!. I saw this line as well and decided not to give him the pleasure.

37...♔g7 38.♘f5+

38...♔g8 Ha-ha.
39.♘h6+ ♔g7 40.♘f5+ gxf5 41.♕h5 ♘g6 White resigned.

A clean game by Peter, who took a bunch of excellent decisions throughout the game. One loss is by no means the end of a match, but I failed to come back. Some luck would have definitely helped, but it turned out that this was it for me in Baku.

Peter Svidler

At first Peter Svidler was playing his usual role of Mr. Nice Guy, but after he had overcome an obstacle as major as Topalov in Round 4, the tone of his interviews changed and the seven-time Russian Champion revealed that he was all set to qualify for the Candidates'. When I was preparing for my encounter with Peter in the semi-finals, I noticed that he had done a lot of work recently. With all the banter blitz he has been doing for *Chess24* one might be fooled to believe that he was on his way to his retirement, but this is very much not the case. It is remarkable how well Peter hides his ambitions. He means business and now he is in the Candidates' 2016.

The other semi-final was played between Sergey Karjakin and Pavel Eljanov.

Sergey Karjakin

The winner of the World Cup. Sergey had to fight for survival from as early as Round 2. He lost his first game with the black pieces against Alexander Onischuk and then had to come back with White against the solid American – not an easy task, considering the psychological pressure, but Sergey handled it impressively.

NOTES BY
Anish Giri

RL 7.1 – C48
Sergey Karjakin
Alexander Onischuk
Baku 2015 (2.2)

1.e4 e5 2.♘f3 ♘c6 3.♗b5 ♘f6
I remember some dubious Spanish games from Onischuk in the past, but in a must-draw situation, the ever solid Berlin seemed like an excellent choice. The disadvantage is that Sergey, being an expert on this subject, knows a lot of tricky little sidelines.
4.d3 ♗c5 5.♘c3!?

5...a6
I am not going to say what I think Black should do here, but this is definitely not the best.
6.♗xc6 dxc6 7.♘xe5!
This and the following sequence look completely harmless, but either Sergey knew what he was doing or he managed to calculate the position much more deeply than one normally would.

7...♕d4 8.♗e3 ♕xe5 9.d4 ♕e7 10.dxc5 ♘xe4

This position reminded me of Carlsen-Alekseev, played back in the day when there were still more than two players who weren't scared of the Viking. There Black had played ...0-0

instead of ...a6, and although Magnus kept trying forever, he not only failed to win, but even managed to lose. Ironically, he was the first one to congratulate Karjakin on his comeback on Twitter. There were more tweets from Magnus during the World Cup, though, and some quite personal ones, too...
11.♕d4 ♗f5 12.0-0-0 0-0 13.♘xe4 ♕xe4

The desire of the defender to exchange as many pieces as possible (especially queens!) is understandable, but the weakness of the c7-pawn will soon begin to tell.
14.♕xe4 ♗xe4 15.f3 ♗f5 16.♗f4 ♖ac8 17.♖he1 ♗e6 18.♖e3 ♖fe8 19.♖d4

If the World Cup is a real-life demonstration of the survival of the fittest, then Sergey Karjakin was a cat with nine lives, stubbornly fighting back and hanging on till the sweet end.

19...b6 Alekseev went ...b5 at some point in this structure, but the queens were still on the board. I am pretty sure Magnus (whom I talk about too much in this game) would prefer to get into the bunker with 19...♖e7!? 20.♖b4 ♖b8, and the question is how Sergey would have attempted to break this. In fact, I am rather surprised that Onischuk didn't go here. On the other hand, sitting and waiting, dreaming of your draw, might feel somewhat miserable, too.

20.♖b4 a5 This might seem like an improvement of Black's pawn structure, but in fact White now has a clear idea: to go c4, take on b6 and get the next pawn to c5.

21.♖a4 ♖e7 22.c4

22...♖d7 22...♖a8 defends against the main threat, but allows 23.b4!?, when Black is still under pressure.
23.cxb6 cxb6 24.c5 bxc5 25.♖xa5

The transformation of the pawn structure is by no means fatal for Black. Yes, White has an outside passer, but the weakness is gone. From this point on, though, Alexander Onischuk starts playing very poorly.
25...c4?
Ugly and bad. 25...♖cd8! was too natural not to be played. Black should use the momentum and grab the d-file: 26.♖e1 h6, and it's very hard for White to make any progress.
26.♖ea3!

Now White can always exchange a pair of rooks, neutralizing any potential counterplay.
26...♖dd8
Compare this to 25... ♖cd8!.
27.♖a7 h6 28.♖c7!?
Exchanging the rooks.
28...♖xc7 29.♗xc7 ♖d3 30.♖a8+ ♔h7 31.♗a5!

A very beautiful set-up. The bishop locks the queenside on c3 and the a-pawn gets carte blanche.
31...h5 32.h4!

Always nice.
32...♗f5?
In this kind of position, *any* action has to be all-out. Something like

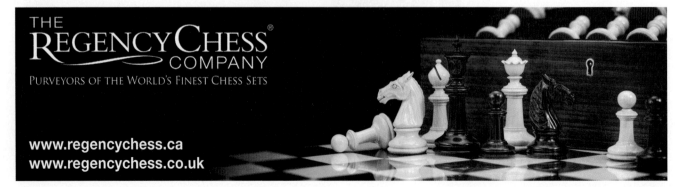

THE **REGENCYCHESS®** COMPANY
PURVEYORS OF THE WORLD'S FINEST CHESS SETS

www.regencychess.ca
www.regencychess.co.uk

32...♖e3!? 33.♔d2 ♖d3+ 34.♔e2
♖d4! 35.♗e1 (35.a4!?) 35...c3! 36.bxc3
♗c4+! would have created some
counterplay.

Perhaps White would have had to
give the h4-pawn, and then there is at
least some hope. Maybe the counterplay would have been just in time?
33.a4 ♖d6 34.♗c3 c5 35.a5 ♖g6
This is far too late.
36.a6 ♖xg2

37.♖f8! 37.a7 would have complicated matters: 37...♖g1+ 38.♔d2 ♖a1,
and it's no longer clear how White
should proceed.
37...♗e6 37...♖g1+ is no longer in
time: 38.♔d2 ♖a1 39.♖xf7.
**38.a7 ♗d5 39.a8♕ ♗xa8
40.♖xa8 ♖f2 41.♖c8**

Black could have continued, for
example with 41...♖h2, but Onischuk
decided that there was no point and
resigned. Indeed, White is completely
winning.

After this Sergey won the tiebreak and
he quickly got the taste of winning
tiebreaks, as he seemed more than
content with 1-1 against Andreikin,
Mamedyarov and Eljanov, not exert-

ing any pressure as White and holding his own with the black pieces. In
the tiebreaks he was an iron man.

Beating Eljanov was a major
achievement in this tournament, and
as a reward Sergey earned his spot in
the Candidates'.

Pavel Eljanov

The Ukrainian grandmaster was per-
forming miracles, winning his first
six games; an incredible feat. He was
not entirely without luck, though, in
his Black game against Grischuk.

With White, however, Pavel
destroyed Grischuk confidently,
and it was only the solid Jakovenko
who managed to hold Pavel to two
draws. That didn't help, though, as
Pavel struck once again, this time in
the tiebreak. Next on the menu was
Hikaru Nakamura. It usually doesn't
get much harder than that.

NOTES BY
Pavel Eljanov

CA 5.12 — E06
Pavel Eljanov
Hikaru Nakamura
Baku 2015 (5.1)

**1.d4 d5 2.♘f3 ♘f6 3.c4 e6
4.g3 ♗e7 5.♗g2 0-0 6.0-0 dxc4
7.♕c2 a6 8.a4 ♗d7 9.♕xc4 ♗c6
10.♗g5 ♗d5 11.♕c2 ♗e4**

12.♕c1!? A rather rare move nowadays, although in my view very logical: White exerts pressure on the
c-file and hinders the typical ...c7-c5.

My opponent has played this line quite
successfully with the white pieces, as
you can read in Anish Giri's notes to
his methodical win against Leko.

This game reminded me of another,
played in 1980 in Amsterdam (it was
some time before Anish appeared on
this earth) – Ribli-Karpov. I also did
not yet exist then, but thanks to books
I learned about this textbook game,
won by the Hungarian grandmaster.
In general it can be said that Black
seemingly should not experience
problems in the modern classical
Catalan, but in recent times White
has won quite a number of games
here. This indicates that Black is
often obliged to solve practical problems (not always successfully). At the
same time, White normally has a very
clear line of play. (A few years ago the
witty Sasha Grischuk said that to play
the Catalan with White it is sufficient
to have one convolution of the brain.)
**12...h6 13.♗xf6 ♗xf6 14.♖d1 a5
15.♘bd2**

15...♗h7 A quite logical novelty –
Black simply does not want to part
with the two bishops.

15...♗xf3 is the most critical move,
since then a very typical structure
for this variation is reached. In the
last round of the super-tournament
in Biel this year, against Adams I had
an identical structure and arrange-
ment of the pieces. I managed to out-
play Mickey and reach a winning
position – only to blunder a couple of
pawns and a rook.
16.♘b3 c6 17.♕c3
I have to exert pressure on the
a5-pawn, since otherwise Black will

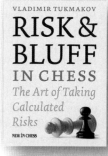
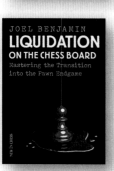

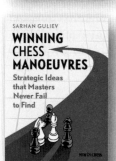

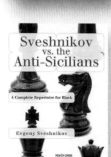

transfer his knight to b4 and will altogether have no problems.

17...♗e7 18.♘c5 ♕c7 19.♘e5 ♘a6

20.♘xb7! The only possibility of fighting for an advantage.

20...♕xb7 21.♗xc6

21...♕c7? This would appear to be Black's only serious mistake in the game. Hikaru thought for a long time, but was unable to choose the best path: 21...♕a7 22.♗xa8 ♗b4!. I thought that all the same White should have ways to gain an advantage, but analysis shows that Black is able to defend: 23.♕f3 ♕xa8 (23...♖xa8?? 24.♘c6) 24.♕xa8 ♖xa8 25.♖ac1 ♗e4! (it is very important to switch the bishop for the defence of the queenside) 26.♘c6 ♗d5 27.♘xb4 ♘xb4 28.♖c3 ♗c6 29.♖c5 ♔f8 30.♖dc1 ♖a6. It is doubtful whether White can breach this defence.

22.♗xa8 ♕xc3 23.bxc3 ♖xa8 24.♘c6! ♗d8 25.♘xd8 ♖xd8 26.f3! Now, apart from the fact that White has the more flexible pawn structure, the black bishop has no great future. At the present moment White does not have access to the b-file, but this

Pavel Eljanov could look back on a sensational performance. The Ukrainian GM won his first six games, gained 35.6 rating points and shot up from 32nd to 13th place in the Live Ratings.

factor is not so important and in the game I managed to regroup and gain control of this file.

26...♖c8 27.♖a3

27...♗g6 It is hard to suggest anything concrete for Black. It is logical to bring up the king with 27...♔f8 28.♔f2 ♔e7, but I do not need to rush with con-

crete play and can first strengthen my position on the kingside with 29.g4! ♘c7 30.e4 ♖b8 31.h4 and all the same White's advantage is obvious.

28.♔f2 ♖b8 29.♖d2 f6

30.♖aa2! Now, when the black king is far away, this invasion gains in strength.

30...♖b3 31.♖ab2 ♖xc3 32.♖b5 ♗c2 33.♖xa5 ♘c7 34.♖a7

34...f5
Here it is already too late for 34...♔f8 35.a5 ♝a4 (or 35...♔e8 36.♖b7 ♔d8 37.d5 exd5 38.a6 ♘xa6 39.♖xd5+ ♔c8 40.♖xg7, winning) 36.♖b7 ♝b5 37.e4 ♝a6 38.♖b6, winning.

35.a5 ♔h7 36.♖b7 ♖c4 37.♖b6 ♝a4 38.a6 ♝c6 39.a7 ♝d5 40.♖a2 ♖xd4 41.♖c2 ♘a8 42.♖a6

Black has managed to set up a last line of defence. But as a rule such positions cannot be held, as I was able to demonstrate in practice.

42...♖d1

43.h4!
Typical play on the principle of two weaknesses. Black cannot allow 44.h5, but at the same time the alternatives are also bad.

43...h5
Both 43...♔g6 44.♖c8 ♝b7 45.♖xe6+ ♔f7 46.♖ce8 and 43...g5 44.h5 ♔g7 45.♖b2 lose as well.

44.♔e3 ♖g1 45.♔f4 ♖g2 46.♖d6 ♖g1 47.♖c8 ♖a1

48.♔g5
There was also another way to win: 48.♖xd5 exd5 49.♖xa8 ♔g6 50.♔e5 ♖a5 51.e3 ♔h7 52.♔d6 ♔g6 53.♔c6,

when the threat of 54.♔b6 leaves Black no choice, and he has to give up his d5-pawn: 53...♖a1 54.♔xd5, winning.

48...♖xa7 49.♖dd8 g6

50.♖h8+
Of course, it would have been more pleasant to conclude with mate in four moves, but to be honest I did not even consider the alternative 50.♔f6! ♔h6 51.♖h8+ ♔h7 52.♖cg8 ♖xh8 53.♖xh8 mate.
The continuation in the game also promises an advantage: about 5 in computer units, which is also not bad.
50...♔g7 51.♖cg8+ ♔f7 52.♖xg6 ♖a6 53.♖h7+ ♔f8 54.♔xh5 ♘b6 55.♔g5 ♘c4 56.h5 ♘d6 57.♖f6+ ♔g8 58.♖d7
Black resigned.

■ ■ ■

As we already know, Pavel's triumphs ended with his match against Karjakin. He gave it a good shot, but the other guy was much luckier.

Final or Postscript
In fact, the main goal for most of the players in the World Cup was qualifying for the Candidates'. Once this had been achieved and two players had reached the final and earned these coveted spots, much of the intrigue had basically gone. However, in this case the two finalists, Karjakin and Svidler, decided to treat us to a spectacular show, with the final score being the binary 0011100111. I watched the first three games, but at some point I could no longer handle it. For this report I had to go through

all the games anyway. Let me guide you through a rollercoaster the likes of which we have seldom if ever seen. I have carefully selected a number of examples to give you an idea what the players and the online spectators went through during four classical games, two rapid games (25 minutes + 10 seconds increment), two semi-rapid games (10 minutes + 10 seconds) and two blitz games (5 minutes + 3 seconds).

Baku 2015
7 rounds of knock-out

Round 3	
Topalov-Lu Shanglei	2½-1½
Nepomniachtchi-Nakamura	4-5
Caruana-Kovalyov	1½-½
Leko-Giri	½-1½
So-Le Quang Liem	2½-1½
Andreikin-Kramnik	2½-1½
Grischuk-Eljanov	0-2
Guseinov-Ding Liren	½-1½
Areshchenko-Wei Yi	½-1½
Ivanchuk-Jakovenko	½-1½
Karjakin-Yu Yangyi	1½-½
Vachier-Lagrave-Tomashevsky	4-2
Granda Zuniga-Wojtaszek	½-1½
Mamedyarov-Sethuraman	1½-½
Adams-Dominguez Perez	5-3
Radjabov-Svidler	1½-2½

Round 4	
Svidler-Topalov	1½-½
Nakamura-Adams	1½-½
Mamedyarov-Caruana	1½-½
Giri-Wojtaszek	3-1
Vachier-Lagrave-So	1½-½
Andreikin-Karjakin	1½-2½
Jakovenko-Eljanov	1½-2½
Ding Liren-Wei Yi	2½-3½

Round 5 Quarterfinals	
Svidler-Wei Yi	3½-2½
Eljanov-Nakamura	1½-½
Mamedyarov-Karjakin	2-4
Vachier-Lagrave-Giri	½-1½

Round 6 Semifinals	
Giri-Svidler	½-1½
Eljanov-Karjakin	2½-3½

Final	
Svidler-Karjakin	4-6

In the second classical game Svidler took a 2-0 lead, after he had won a nicely conducted first game. How did Sergey make sure Peter went two up?

Karjakin-Svidler
Baku 2015 (7.2)
position after 36...♕c6

The position two moves before the end of the game. At some point White will take the pinned rook on f7 and the resulting endgame should be a draw. But Sergey finds almost the only move to lose!
37.♖b5?? ♔h8! And as the bishop defends the rook on b5, White is suddenly a full piece down. Black still would have some work to do, but White makes his life easier by immediately dropping another piece.
38.♖d5?? ♘b6 White resigned.

Trailing 0-2, Karjakin needed to win Game 3 to stay in the race. How could Svidler help him?

Svidler-Karjakin
Baku 2015 (7.3)
position after 25.♕e3

Svidler only needs a draw to win the World Cup. Of course, winning the third game would also do.

25...♘xf2?
As if anticipating a blunder, although it's quite an art to find one in such a position. After 25...♕xf2+ 26.♕xf2 ♘xf2 the position would be equal.
26.♖f1 ♕e4 27.♖be1 exd5 28.♖xf2??
The first step towards the abyss. Both 28.♕d2 and 28.♕c3 win for White.
28...♕h4!
After such a move, you'd normally speaking get a very serious adrenaline shock, you turn red, your clothes start to soak and you desperately try to find your way out with your brain working at full capacity. This wasn't what happened here, though.

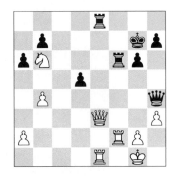

29.♕d2?? And mission accomplished. White could reach a draw with 29.♕xe8 ♕xf2+ 30.♔h2 ♕xb6 31.♖e7+ ♔h6 32.♖d7.
29...♖xf2 30.♕c3+ d4 And White

resigned. An inexplicable turn of events, considering that Svidler still had 14 minutes at this point and the importance of the moment.

The rapid games did not bring a decision either. First Svidler lost Game 5, but he struck back with a positional masterpiece in Game 6.

On to the semi-rapid games! Here's Game 7. How can White be worse against the Benoni in 10 moves?

KI 80.11 E61
Sergey Karjakin
Peter Svidler
Baku 2015 (7.7)
1.♘f3 ♘f6 2.c4 c5 3.e3 g6 4.d4 ♗g7 5.d5 0-0 6.♘c3 d6 7.h3 e6 8.♗e2

8...♖e8 9.♘d2 ♘a6 10.dxe6

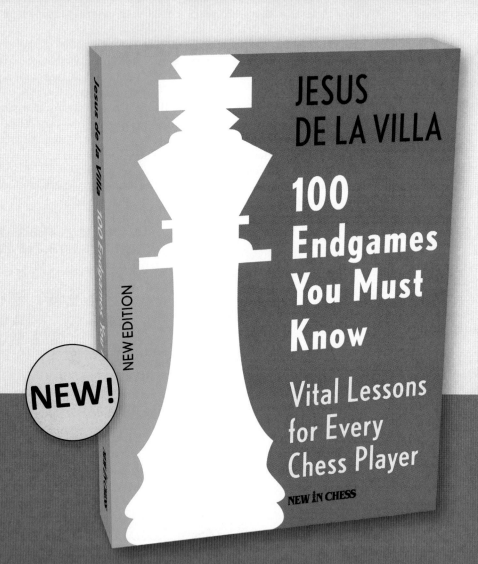

'The horror'. **10...♗xe6 11.0-0 d5 12.cxd5 ♘xd5 13.♘xd5 ♗xd5** Black is already much better.

14.♕c2 ♘b4 15.♕b1 ♕e7 16.a3 ♘c6 17.a4 ♕e6 18.♖a3 c4 19.♖e1 ♖ad8 20.a5 ♘f8 21.♖a4 ♘e5 22.e4 ♗c6

23.♖xc4? Oh well, why not? **23...♖xd2** That's why. **24.♗xd2 ♘xc4** And White was completely lost.

25.♗c3 ♘d6 26.f3 ♗g7 27.♗xg7 ♔xg7 28.♕d3 ♕e5 29.♕d2 a6 30.♖d1 ♘b5 31.♕b4 ♘c7 32.♕b6 f5 33.♗d3 ♖d8 34.exf5 gxf5 35.♔f2 ♕d4+ 36.♕xd4+ ♖xd4 37.♔e3 ♘e6 38.♖c1 f4+ 39.♔e2 ♖b4 40.♗xa6 bxa6 White resigned.

Game 8 was another smooth comeback by Karjakin, and then it was time for the blitz games. Game 9 featured a widely known (in narrow circles) position and a very critical one as well. How does one make a mess of it?

RL 17.4 – C89
Sergey Karjakin
Peter Svidler
Baku 2015 (7.9)

1.e4 e5 2.♘f3 ♘c6 3.♗b5 a6 4.♗a4 ♘f6 5.0-0 ♗e7 6.♖e1 b5 7.♗b3 0-0 8.c3 d5 9.exd5 ♘xd5 10.♘xe5 ♘xe5 11.♖xe5 c6 12.d3 ♗d6 13.♖e1 ♗f5 14.♕f3 ♖e8 15.♖xe8+ ♕xe8 16.♘d2 ♕e1+ 17.♘f1 ♗g6

My database counts 74 games with this position and I am afraid to count the amount of engine games. Miracles begin to happen though.
18.♗c2?? b4?? 18...♘xc3! would have been game over for White. **19. c4** Now White is clearly better, but not for very long. **19...b3 20.♗d1 ♘b4 21.♗d2 ♕e5 22.♗c3 ♕c5 23.♗xb4 ♕xb4 24.♗xb3 ♕b6 25.♖e1 ♗c5 26.♗a4 ♖d8 27.♖d1 ♕xb2 28.♗xc6 ♗h5**

29.♖b1?? This move is losing for at least five reasons. But 29.g4 wins: 29...♗xg4 30.♕xg4 ♕xf2+ 31.♔h1 and there is no mate. **29...♕xb1** One reason. The other four reasons were 29...♗xf3, 29...♗xf2+, 29...♕xa2 and 29...♕c2. **30.♕xh5 ♗xf2+ 31.♔xf2 ♕b6+ 32.♘e3 ♕xc6 33.♘d5 ♕d6 34.g3 h6 35.♕e2 ♖b8 36.♔g2 ♔h8 37.h4 ♕a3 38.♔h3 ♕c1 39.♘f4 ♕b2 40.♕e7 ♕b7 41.♕e5 ♕d7+ 42.♔h2** Black still has good winning chances, but...

42...♔g8?? 43.♕xb8+ Say what? Black resigned.

By now we thought we had figured it all out and were all certain that Svidler was going to come back in Game 10. Or was he? Nope! He lost and so Sergey Karjakin took the Cup! In Svidler's words at the final press conference:

'Basically the recipe for solving the drawing problem in chess is very simple – you take two reasonably strong players, you make them completely exhausted and then you make them play a long match. And you will get results, as you have all seen. But I don't think this match is in any way representative of the future of chess, or even the present of chess. It was just a bit of a circus in the Roman sense of the word. The lions either won or lost. It's up to the public to decide whether the lions won or lost. It was a very specific set of circumstances.'

Congratulations to the lions, but let's hope this is not the future of chess. ∎

Strange as it may sound, it took many years before I realised that chess magazines could be collected. Monthlies were ephemera – perishables, to be tossed away like mouldy loaves of bread. As a consequence, I can no longer recall with precision which publications comprised my formative reading. B.H. Wood's *Chess* was certainly among them, though, with its endless adverts for books, sets and tawdry, acrylic ties. Little did I know it had begun its life with highbrow annotations by the likes of Alekhine, and theoretical surveys by Euwe. Later, when my team, Atherton, would occasionally drive down to Wood's veritable Aladdin's Cave of chess merchandise at Sutton Coldfield (a convenient Midlands location) for matches in the National Club Championship, my emotional bond with his flagship periodical strengthened.

In comparison, the grand old dame, British Chess Magazine, appeared a touch fusty. However, with an acquisitiveness born of middle-age and increasing affluence, I have since procured over a hundred volumes of this venerable journal, which perhaps allows a better appraisal of its merit. Sadly, this once esteemed gazette has barely crawled into the 21st century, on life-support and with reputation threadbare, but, for much of its long existence, with its donnish prose, historical articles and news from distant dominions, it was a very fine read.

One oddity surfacing from this trip down memory lane was that for a time – perhaps a year or two – I received a subscription to a Russian newspaper, which I guess must have been '64', because it also contained draughts. There is not a chance in a million that anyone in my family would have thought of this, so I can only assume it was either on the initiative of the left-leaning Oxonian, Leonard Barden, who was in charge of junior chess at that time, or, more likely, Bob Wade, who, among countless other ill-paying jobs, had once written the chess column for the Kremlin-backed *Daily Worker* (taking over from the Communist former British Champion, William Winter). Presumably, the generous idea was that when the inevitable dictatorship of the proletariat came, my expert knowledge of the language of Tolstoy would stand me in good stead. Regrettably, possessing neither a dictionary nor linguistic talent, I never progressed much beyond deciphering the names.

In the September of 1984, New In Chess presented itself to the world. Yes, my dear innumerate employers, that was 31 years ago, and not 30. Anyway, arithmetic deficiencies aside, it has remained my favourite magazine ever since. For someone with such fond, nostalgic yearnings, perusing the early issues, however, can be a slight disappointment. It is analogous to hearing a popular tune from your youth on the radio and suddenly realising it wasn't quite as good as you had remembered it. Perhaps I have become finicky in middle-age. For example, while the quality of production has never been shoddy, it was a far cry from today's slick professionalism.

The contents have steadily improved too. I remember Bent Larsen, at my flat in London in 1991, tossing away a copy of some short-lived publication, which had popped through my mailbox that morning, with the contemptuous remark 'Another worthless magazine with unannotated games!' The Dane was far-sighted. Game-scores – once a prized commodity – have fallen victim in the era of gargantuan databases to the economics of proliferation. Without lucid exposition to accompany it, the naked record of moves has almost zero value. In general, New In Chess has been rather successful in securing the authorship of top players. I have sometimes felt that I could learn more about the King's Indian from a single Kramnik game, effortlessly explained, than from an entire week of my own study. But in those early days one could often find bland, Informator-style, wordless scores and, worse still, even Larsen's reviled 'nudes'.

As befitted a journal emanating from the Netherlands, it had (and to some degree retains) a Dutch bias. This was, arguably, less a reflection of inherent parochialism than recognition of the country's deep chess culture and status as the most important venue for elite events. Both as a protagonist and a renowned analyst, Jan Timman was always worth reading, although the harsh, cold scrutiny of engines inevitably takes the gloss off the latter over time. I still especially enjoy his explorations into the field of studies. Jan's mantle as player-author has, however, effectively been taken up by Anish Giri, whose lighter, more humorous style captures the zeitgeist of the social-media generation. From the stalwarts, the opinionated Hans Ree bristles with erudition and self-assuredness, even if his polemical manner tends to rub up a few people the wrong way. By contrast, Genna Sosonko, with his mastery of the short, biographical portrait, is silky smooth. Others have come

DIRTY MAGS

and gone – not always with regret – but I do sometimes miss the quirky Tim Krabbé.

At the risk of sounding oleaginous, New In Chess is a superb chronicle of an epoch – a vade mecum, if you will. It was almost inevitable that your writer would hold a strongly personal identification with it, because the lifespan of this Anglophone periodical, with its emphasis on top international chess, more or less coincides exactly with my time as a grandmaster. Indeed, the very first issue contained a report by Ray Keene on my victory in the British Championship. And, for better or worse, I have rarely been out of the pages for any prolonged period of time since.

My own literary contributions, though, were initially brief and infrequent – an occasional game annotation here or there – but under the benign encouragement of the exalted editor, these gradually expanded into lengthier tournament reports. Only with the arrival of the larger page format, in January 2011, did the free-ranging and oft-provocative 'Short Stories' become a regular feature. I was proud to discover, from a massive online survey a while back, that I am simultaneously the most popular and unpopular writer in the magazine – although how much of the latter is due to the multiple accounts/personalities of Paul Truong I know not. Anyway, there are few things worse than being ignored. Flatteringly, dozens of subscribers, including not a few strong grandmasters, use these two pages to diligently improve their English vocabulary – a thorough, scholarly method of which the quinquesyllabic Russian theoretician, Polugaevsky, would undoubtedly have approved.

Magazines should be either fun or informative, or preferably both – which is presumably why Robert Hübner has a large collection of Asterix comics in various languages. What better way to note the nuances of a tongue than by following the exploits of the plucky Gaul and his menhir-wielding chum? Actually, the German papyrologist is primarily responsible for instilling my love of chess periodicals. When I played for Solingen in the Bundesliga back in the 1980s, I used to stay at his flat. What those weekends lacked in culinary comfort were more than compensated by witty conversation and earnest discussion. I also had free run of his excellent library. While I was more awed than enamoured with his rows of Deutsche Schachzeitung, other obscurer tomes piqued my interest. I discovered that Johannes Zukertort's analysis of the Italian Game in – was it? – the Westminster Papers in the 1870s was in some respects superior to a certain well-known Yugoslav encyclopaedia a century later. This came as a revelation, for up until that point I had always assumed that chess knowledge invariably expanded. It usually does, of course, but it can also occasionally contract.

These days I could dispense with my entire pile of openings monographs with barely a tinge of regret. They have about the same value as a sandwich, but without the shelf-life. No – give me biographies, games collections, histories, tournament books, but above all lovingly bound magazines. English is preferred, but any language that I can stumble my way through will suffice. Incidentally Schaakbulletin – the precursor of this esteemed publication – was well worth a glance.

The latest addition to my groaning bookcases is Cecil Purdy's Australasian Chess Review or Chess World of which I picked up numerous volumes when I was in Melbourne last year. The first World Correspondence Champion had such an admirable way of explaining games and expressing ideas with great clarity that it is no wonder that Bobby Fischer held him in high regard. I was also amused to find two articles in which, building upon Emanuel Lasker's earlier criticisms, he argued forcefully against the absurdity of stalemate being a draw. I was unaware of this antipodean antecedent when I proposed the identical rule change in New In Chess 2012/6, page 75.

Now that this column draws to an end, my appetite has been whetted for a little reading. What should it be? A bucolic stroll through the ovine pastures of New Zealand Chess perhaps? No, I will save that for late December, when I fly to Auckland. I want something spicier for now. The International Chess Magazine, maybe? Yes, the poison-tipped quill of Wilhelm Steinitz should do just fine. Besides, I need to hone my skills for the next time I write about the dunderheads and buffoons who regrettably preside over our game. ∎

Nakamura shows stamina in Vegas

In the final of the 2nd Millionaire Chess Open Hikaru Nakamura defeated Le Quang Liem to take home the $100,000 winner's check.

Robert Hess

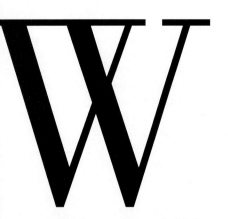

What better place to hold the open chess tournament with the world's biggest purse than a city that greets you with slot machines and scantily clad individuals? Las Vegas' Planet Hollywood housed the 2nd Millionaire Chess Open in the second week of October, as nearly 600 competitors from roughly 50 countries flocked the Grand Ballroom, which was adorned in MCO's trademark royal purple. Although all competitors had to fork over a pricy entry fee (at the earliest deadline, it was $1,000), the tournament featured 36 GMs. The class sections were filled with talented amateurs, who were fighting to win enormous paydays. Where else can a player rated below master level win prizes exceeding $30,000?

Joining Wesley So on the top boards this year were the defending champion's compatriots Hikaru Nakamura and Fabiano Caruana, the world's second and sixth rated players, respectively. The storyline wrote itself as the top three American players were set to duke it out for a whopping $100,000 grand prize. Unlike most Opens, which have a traditional nine-round schedule and all participants remain in the same field for the entire event, Millionaire Chess has spiced things up by introducing Millionaire Monday; in all sections, there is a 7-round sprint, after which the top four scorers battle one another in elimination matches for the top prize. At Millionaire, there can only be *one* winner.

But Millionaire Chess is about far more than just the chess, as Maurice Ashley and Amy Lee continue to strive for chess to reach a mainstream audience. The ever-dedicated organizers super-sized the second edition, hosting a pool party, providing a free opening breakfast and lectures, and staging a red carpet photo shoot with the official tournament photographer David Llada. The confessional booth was a resounding success, allowing fans to hear the often hilarious thoughts of competitors of all playing abilities. And, obviously, with so much money at stake, there were strict anti-cheating measures.

As for the action on the board, the tournament was a classy affair. After three rounds, it was clear that Caruana remained in shaky form, as the former world number two stumbled

PHOTOS: DAVID LLADA

GM Maurice Ashley and entrepreneur Amy Lee super-sized the second edition of Millionaire Chess. WGM Tania Sachdev and GM Robert Hess entertained the Internet audience. And who won? A happy Hikaru Nakamura!

to two consecutive draws against players rated roughly 350 points below him. Caissa continued to bless Ray Robson, last year's runner-up, as he escaped Alex Fishbein's clutches and remained perfect. Luck was not on Gata Kamsky's side, as the five-time US Champion actually forfeited his game for showing up just two minutes after the 30-minute grace period had elapsed.

In Round 4, Wesley So, who up to that point had seemed invincible, hit a roadblock in the form of Azeri GM and Webster University student Vasif Durarbayli, whose defensive prowess enthralled us commentators. The tournament situation had become clearer, as Le Quang Liem, Yu Yangyi, and Evgeny Bareev joined Durarbayli as the only unscathed players.

Three rounds later, Le, Yu, and Aleksander Lenderman – an improving American grandmaster who ended Ray Robson's run by soundly defeating him with the black pieces – were assured of their qualification with six points each. There was quite a bit of controversy in Round 7, when Nakamura and England's Luke McShane agreed to a draw by repetition in just nine moves, 21 moves earlier than allowed in MCO. Maurice Ashley despised the decision, suggesting that, despite understanding their rationale for doing so, these incredibly gifted fighters continued a practice that harms chess' image. After

97 minutes of communicating with FIDE officials and arbiters all around the world, the result was upheld.

Including McShane, a rat pack of nine players with 5½/7 were forced into a playoff consisting of two distinct round-robin groups playing 25-minute games with a 5-second delay. The first included So, Caruana, Aleksandr Shimanov, Gregory Kaidanov, and McShane. The group saw Nakamura take on challengers Kamsky, Evgeny Bareev (now playing for Canada and a face chess fans were happy to see drawn out of retirement. And a man who had a chance to qualify directly but squandered a winning position against Sam Shankland in the seventh round), and Sergei Azarov. Nakamura managed to get past Kamsky in blitz tiebreakers, while So steamrolled through his group, with a clinching victory over Shimanov in the fourth game. Hikaru and Wesley then met in a three game, 15-minutes per player rapid match, which the American number one won after surviving difficult (perhaps lost) posi-

> 'The confessional booth was a resounding success, allowing fans to hear the often hilarious thoughts of the competitors.'

tions in the first two games before returning to vintage Nakamura form in a convincing victory with White.

And the rest is history. Nakamura, benefitting from his recent experience in the World Cup in Baku, once again survived a scare, this time overcoming Yu Yangyi 2½-1½, while Le Quang Liem soundly defeated Lenderman 2-0. In the finals, Nakamura played his best game of the tournament (see below) before graciously allowing Le a half point in a winning position for the American. And, just like that, Nakamura became $100,000 richer. Le took home $50,000, while Yu once against had to settle for third place and $25,000. For his efforts, Lenderman was also rewarded handsomely, taking home a cool $16,000.

As the slogan goes, what happens in Vegas, stays in Vegas. Typically that includes your gambled money, but luckily for the winners at the second Millionaire Chess Open, you're not allowed to buy chips with checks.

NOTES BY
Robert Hess

QO 16.6 – D30
Hikaru Nakamura
Le Quang Liem
Las Vegas 2015 (2)

Nakamura and Le had just eliminated Yu Yangyi and Aleks Lenderman, respectively. Now these two super grandmasters were competing for the Millionaire Chess title, with the winner receiving a payday double that of the runner-up.
1.d4 ♘f6 2.c4 e6 3.♘f3 d5 4.♗g5 h6 5.♗xf6 ♕xf6 6.♕b3

Nakamura opts for the early queen sortie rather than entering the Hastings Variation (6.♘c3 c6 7.♕b3). In a rapid game, this proved a wise practical choice, as it allowed the American player to avoid main lines and force Le to find an adequate defensive setup.
6...c6
6...dxc4 might have been timely. If 7.♕xc4 ♗d6 8.e4 e5, Black is not

behind in development and seems to have a solid position.
7.e3 ♕e7 8.♘bd2 ♕b4 9.♕c2

Le's queen's adventures have come to a halt, and Nakamura's lead in development and spatial advantage give him a clear plus.
9...♘d7 10.a3 ♕a5 11.♗e2 dxc4
Releasing the tension, and for no good reason. 11...♗e7 12.0-0 0-0 would have made Nakamura's task less straightforward. The knight on d2 would remain at bay and how White turns his lead in development into something a little more concrete is less certain.
12.0-0

12...♗e7

Dubious was 12...b5?! 13.b3 ♖b8 (13...♗e7 14.a4) 14.bxc4 ♗e7 15.cxb5 cxb5 16.d5! exd5 17.♘d4 and for the cost of just a pawn, White has achieved positional dominance.
13.♘xc4 ♕c7 14.b4 0-0 15.♖ac1 ♖d8 16.♕b3

16...a6 Nakamura has been playing perfectly, although the position is quite easy to play as White. Le should have considered an attempt to gain space on the queenside by playing 16...b6 17.♘ce5 (17.♘fe5 ♗a6 18.♘xd7 ♖xd7 19.♖fe1 is also clearly better for White) 17...c5 18.♘xd7 ♗xd7 19.♘e5 a5! . Black might drop a pawn, but at least his pieces can breathe.
17.♗d3 ♘f6 18.♗b1

Millionaire Chess Open   Date _October 12, 2015_
Pay to the Order of _KHASEN LEVKIN_ $30,000.00
Thirty Thousand Dollars
For _1st Place - Under 1600_

Where else can an under-1600 player win $30,000? Khasen Levkin cried as he revealed that he was going to send the money to his mom and grandma back in Russia.

18...♗d7 Once again, Black is at a crossroads. The choice is between being solid with no space or attempting to lash out and potentially lose a pawn. It generally is easier to fight for survival when you have some activity, whereas moves like ...♗d7 just prolong the positional suffering. Although 18...b6 19.♘ce5 c5 20.♘d3 ♗b7 21.bxc5 bxc5 22.♘xc5 ♗xf3 23.gxf3 ♖ab8 is no fun for Black, Le would have some chances here, especially in a rapid game.
19.e4 ♗e8 20.e5

20...♘h7? 20...♘d5 was a better choice. Black can't afford to continue retreating. White's attack does not yet have venom, so putting the knight in the centre would have been more sensible: 21.h4 h5 22.♘g5 g6 . This is anything but pretty for Black, but it is also not at all clear how White plans to break through.
21.♕e3 b6 22.♖fd1 a5

22...♘g5 23.♘e1 a5 24.h4 ♘h7 also falls victim to the exact same tactic as was played in the game.

23.d5! ♖xd5 Le could have put up more stubborn resistance with 23...cxd5 24.♘xb6 ♕b7 25.♘xa8 ♖xa8, after which Nakamura is up an exchange, but the resulting position is far from easy to convert.
24.♖xd5 exd5 25.♘xb6 ♖d8 26.♘xd5

The point, which Le did not realize when he went 22... a5. White's knight is immune to capture, for after 26...♖xd5 27.♕e4 ♘f8 28.♕xd5, White is up a clean exchange.
26...♕b7 27.♘xe7+ ♕xe7 28.bxa5 ♖a8 29.a6

Nakamura earns his money with the very same tactic, as the a-pawn is immune since ♕d3 hits the rook and knight once more. As IM Lawrence Trent said in the studio, the two diagonals forms a 'V' for victory.
29...♘f8 30.♗d3 ♘e6 31.♗d4 ♘xd4 32.♕xd4 ♖d8 33.♕c3 c5 34.♗f1 ♖d5 35.♕a5 ♗c6 36.a7 ♗a8 37.♖b1 ♔h7 38.♖b8 c4 39.♕a6 ♖d2 40.♖xa8 ♕c5 41.♖h8+ ♔xh8 42.a8♕+

And Le Quang Liem resigned.
A truly dominating performance by Hikaru Nakamura, who easily held (and indeed was winning) in the second game of the final with the black pieces. ∎

Kings on the attack

The aim of the game is to mate the opponent's king. But the king may bite back, as our new columnist JUDIT POLGAR shows.

The chess king differs in status from the real kings we know from the history books. Far from being a hero, leading its army to victory, our king requires special care and protection. Just think of it: when chess entered Europe, a special rule aimed at teleporting it far from danger was designed: castling!

Yet, the king has a chameleonic character, since in the endgame it can suddenly become an important attacking piece. But the real fun comes when this happens in the middlegame, as in one of my favourite games as a teenager.

instantly. After a few moments of double-checking, he resigned without going all the way to the scaffold: 33...♔xg7 34.♖fxf7+ ♔h6 35.♖h7 mate.

The recent game Navara-Wojtaszek, Biel 2015, (see New In Chess 2015/6) featured a stunning king march from f1 all the way to h8, evoking associations with our theme in its purest form: Short-Timman, Tilburg 1991, when White calmly walked his king up the board from g1 to h6. Or rather to g5, as at that point Black resigned, not awaiting the inevitable checkmate.

In chess, as in real life, nothing is really new, and I was amused to find Nigel's idea in a game played almost 90 years earlier, even though the example is 'imperfect'.

Polgar-L.B.Hansen
Vejstrup Politiken Cup 1989
position after 31...♖e2

32.♔h4!? Lars Bo must have taken this as a desperate attempt to save my king, without noticing that my king's control of g5 creates a deadly threat.
32...♕xg2? 33.♕g7+!
Oops... My opponent's face turned red

Teichmann-Consultants
Glasgow 1902
position after 27.c3

White has almost complete domination, but Black's pressure on g2 prevents the

decisive ♖e2-e3-g3. It is always possible to simplify to a better endgame with ♕e6+, but at the start of the 20th century this was not in the spirit of an exhibition game.
27...h6?! It seems to make sense to prepare an escape hatch for the king on h7, but in fact this move is simply too... inviting!
28.♔h2! Apparently a purely prophylactic move, evacuating the g1-a7 diagonal and thus preparing 29.♖e4 without fearing 29...♕c5+ 30.♔d4 ♖e8!.
28...b5? This might have cost Black a pawn and the game after 29.♕e6+ ♔h8 30.♕xd5 ♖xd5 31.♘xb5. But Teichmann could not resist initiating a heroic plan...
29.♔g3 a5? I would have played 29...♕d1, looking for counter-chances and hoping to make the white king regret having embarked on such a risky adventure.
30.♔h4 White has the double threat of ♔h5-g6 and ♖e3-g3, without fearing ...♕xg2 anymore.
30...g6? Just pointless.
31.♖e3 With the thematic threat of 32.♖g3 g5+ 33.♔h5 ♕e5 34.♖e3! ♕xe7 35.♖xe7 ♖d8 36.♘b7, followed by ♔g6.
31...♕xg2 32.♖g3 ♕f2 33.fxg6 ♕f4+

34.♖g4 Even more than a century ago, players were capable of great accuracy: 34.♔h5? allows an unexpected finish: 34...♗f3+ 35.♖xf3 ♕g5 mate.
34...♕f2+ 35.♔h5 And White won.

Things are even more entertaining when a hunted king becomes the hunter.

Spassky-Tal
Riga 1958
position after 55.♔g3

In the last round of the 1958 Soviet championship, Spassky needed to win to qualify for the Interzonal. A draw would leave Tal in second place after Petrosian. Ever since the adjournment on move 41 it had been very one sided: White tried to mate the black king, which was slipping through his fingers like a wet fish. No one expected Tal to win the game and the championship.

55...h5? Tal hopes to give his king some stability on f5! The idea is correct, but this was not the right moment. Better was 55...♕c7+ 56.♔f2 ♖e6.

56.♔f2! ♖e6

57.♖c8? Missing the fantastic 57.♕b8! (threatening ♖a7 and exploiting the fact that ...♕d6 does not check the king) 57...♔f6 58.g4! (I have won so many games by advancing my g-pawn that I consider g2-g4 (or ...g7-g5) my trademark move, and I always enjoy seeing it) 58...hxg4 59.fxg4 (threatening 60.g5+ ♔f5, and the unexpected retreat

61.♕b3!, with mate in sight) 59...♖e4 60.♕h8+ ♔e7 61.♕f8+ ♔f6 62.♖a6+ ♖e6 63.g5+ ♔f5 and now 64.♕a3!!.

57...♖d6? 58.♕f8+ ♔f6

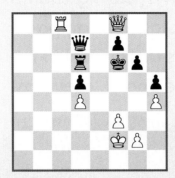

59.♖e8? Again, he should have played the g-pawn: 59.g4! (threatening ♕h8+, followed by g5 or simply ♖e8) 59...hxg4

'I consider g2-g4 (or ...g7-g5) my trademark move, and I always enjoy seeing it.'

60.fxg4 ♖b6 61.♔f3! ♖b3+ 62.♔f4, and Black has no more checks and game over.

59...♖e6 60.♕h8+ ♔f5

Tal has finally achieved the position he had been aiming for with 55...h5. But White's attack continues.

61.♕h6! With the wonderful idea of 61...♖xe8? 62.♕g5+ ♔e6 63.♕e5 mate!

61...♔f6 62.♕h8+ ♔f5 63.♖d8 ♕c6

64.♖c8 ♕a6 Black threatens to win with 65...♕e2+ 66.♔g3 ♕e1+ 67.♔h3 ♕h1+ 68.♔g3 ♖e2.

65.♔g3?! White had several ways of forcing Black to give a perpetual, for instance: 65.♕d8 ♕e2+ 66.♔g3 ♕e1+ 67.♔h3 ♕h1+ 68.♔g3.

65...♕d6+ 66.♔h3 Tal writes that at some point Spassky offered a draw with a pinched voice, but does not say exactly when. It could have been here.

66...♖e1

The initiative has completely passed into Black's hands and Spassky misses the only saving move.

67.g3? Necessary was 67.g4+! hxg4+ 68.fxg4+ ♔f4, when the calm retreat 69.♖c3 saves the game.

67...♖g1 67...♕a6!, threatening ...♖f1+, would have won on the spot.

68.f4 ♖e1 69.♖c2? The only move to stay in the game was 69.♖e8.

69...♕e6!

70.♖f2?! 70.♕c8 ♕xc8 71.♖xc8 still offered some hope. **70...♖h1+ 71.♔g2 ♕e4+ 72.♔f3 ♔g4** The triumph of the black king. **73.♕c8+ f5** 0-1

The moral of the story: the king is not always a comfortable target! ∎

Kasparov, Carlsen and Hou Yifan accepted the invitation, and so did other chess enthusiasts, such as snooker legend Steve Davis, boxing champ Lennox Lewis and football star Sol Campbell. They all came to talk chess (and more) in the BBC Radio 4 series *Across the Board*. Their host (and staunch chess lover) **DOMINIC LAWSON** looks back on the first three seasons.

Radio Days

Chess on the radio? Why not radio snooker as well, a friend mocked, when I told him that I had been signed up by BBC Radio 4 to broadcast a series of chess encounters. It was a natural objection, back in 2013, when the first series of *Across the Board* was being planned. But it was not as crazy as all that. After all, millions of my fellow countrymen are addicted to the BBC radio coverage of Ashes test match cricket.

And I was on strong ground, since the idea was entirely that of the controller of Radio 4, Gwyneth Williams, and she drew a similar comparison in her proposing letter to me: 'Although not much of a chess player, I admire the game; it has entered (like cricket) into the language and culture and it somehow matters.' It somehow matters. We chess fans had been waiting for many decades for a senior executive at the BBC to say something like that about our game. And isn't that the ethos of public service broadcasting?

Actually, I had more doubts than Gwyneth. It's one thing to have a cricket commentator say something like 'and he's struck the ball powerfully to the square leg boundary'. Millions can instantly imagine what that means. But how many listeners would have the appropriate idea in their heads, if I said 'I need to contest the a1-h8 diagonal, so I'm going to bring my bishop back to c1 and then to b2'? Not so many. Yet here's the peculiar thing: when the BBC went through its listener feedback to the first few programmes, it logged many calls along the lines of 'I don't play chess at all, but I really liked it when they gave technical descriptions of the game'. Perhaps it is the same attitude which led many millions to buy Stephen Hawking's *A Brief History of Time*: string theory might remain a mystery to them, but they like the sound of it.

But the moves were really the background to the main content: interviews with a mixture of chess geniuses and eminent people in other fields who have a passion for the game. The plan was to have one of the former and four of the latter in each five-episode series. Surprisingly – to me at least – it was easier to persuade the chess champions to take part: Hou Yifan in series 1, Magnus Carlsen in series 2 and Garry Kasparov in series 3. It was not quite so straightforward getting big names with chess as their publicized hobby to agree.

For example, we got nowhere with the Virgin group founder Sir Richard Branson, not a man normally associated with turning down a challenge. We thought of him because he has a piece on his website with a photo of him playing chess, in which he spoke of how he finds the game 'relaxing and stimulating'. Yet he didn't want to be stimulated over the board for the BBC. Perhaps that photo on his website provides a clue to the real reason. One of the online comments below it reads: 'Here's my big chance to give some publicity advice to Richard Branson... next time you are photographed pretending to play chess make sure the board is not rotated around 90 degrees from its proper orientation. "Light on the right", remember?'

The series producer, David Edmonds, after other similar rebuffs, commented to me that it turns out there 'are loads of celebs who claim they play chess – no doubt to burnish their intellectual credentials – but are unwilling to be put to the test.' I should say here that Dave himself, aside from being a distinguished radio producer – especially of programmes about philosophy – is also a strong chess player. Although he gave up the game many years ago, he was part of the England youth squad of the Nigel Short generation, and was one of a handful of those young lions who beat Vassily Smyslov when the ex-World Champion was ill-advised enough to take a group of them on in a simultaneous exhibition in the UK.

Normally, while doing an interview programme in a BBC studio, it is maddening when the producer in the adjoining glass-walled control room starts making suggestions through your headphones. And in these programmes I was already tasked with concentrating both on the game itself, the clock (half an hour for each player), writing down the moves, asking questions and dealing with the (sometimes surprising) replies to them. Yet I welcomed Dave's interjections through the headphones, as he could always tell when the game was reaching interesting moments, and would then ask me to bring the listener up to date with events at the board.

We didn't always agree on who should be the guests: he was eternally

PHIL COOMES (BBC)

'Perhaps it is the same attitude which led many millions to buy Stephen Hawking's *A Brief History of Time*: string theory might remain a mystery to them, but they like the sound of it.'

Snooker legend (and former president of the British Chess Federation!) Steve Davis and Dominic Lawson avert their eyes as producer David Edmonds tries out an illegal move on their board in the BBC 4 Radio studios.

keen to get models such as the Estonian Carmen Kass and Britain's own Lily Cole into our studio. My objection – that their undoubted beauty hardly recommended itself to a radio audience – did not dampen his enthusiasm. Kass proved elusive and Cole's PR team turned him down repeatedly. Although, having noticed a G-Star interview with Cole (based on her joint fashion shoot with Magnus Carlsen) in which she declared herself to be a regular player – and

having seen a photo of her appearing to play chess with Veselin Topalov – I decided to go up to the model myself when I found her as a fellow guest at a friend's party. Disappointingly, she told me that she could barely play at all – so perhaps in the Branson category.

However, Magnus Carlsen himself had no hesitation in accepting the challenge. We flew out to Norway, where he squeezed us in having just filmed a photo-shoot for a luxury watch magazine. The site was a fabulous hill-side home, and Magnus remarked to me of the shoot that he had just completed: 'I hope I never have to do anything as pretentious as this again'. He then referred sardonically to the view outside as 'Snob Valley.' When we began recording, I set the scene for the radio audience by saying that 'we are playing in the beautiful countryside surrounding Oslo, overlooking Snob Valley.' Listeners would not have been aware of the enormous grin that Magnus immediately flashed – and Dave managed to keep that introduction in the final edit. Fortunately the BBC received no complaints from listeners pointing out that there is no Snob Valley in Oslo.

This little joke might have been why Magnus, who can sometimes be taciturn in interviews, was thoroughly entertaining when answering my questions – as New In Chess readers can discover by going to the BBC i-player. And the game itself? I was crushed, of course. But I do treasure the moment when I played a move and immediately asked a question, to which Magnus responded 'I am going to stop talking now and think about the position, as you have just played the move I feared – but did not expect to see.' A wonderful example of the back-handed compliment.

The conversation was less easy when I interviewed Carlsen's great predecessor Garry Kasparov in the following series. I think this is partly because the former World Champion retains such an aggressive manner at the board that it is difficult for him simultaneously to relax (which is what one wants from a good interviewee). Here is GM Daniel King's description (courtesy of www.chess.co.uk) of what happened. Dan was present during many games: the BBC had hired him to give the listeners objective commentary.

Dominic Lawson-Garry Kasparov

'Dominic's opening was too modest. Garry seized the centre and is now beginning a pawn storm on the king-

> # 'I was surprised when she answered one of my questions with the observation that in chess women had an inherent disadvantage against men.'

side. But here is where the game gets interesting. Sensing that it was 'now or never', Dominic broke out.
18.e5 ♘xe5 19.♘e4...
'At this moment I could see Garry tense up. He hunched over the board, his answers became more terse and he began shaking his twisted feet under the table. Moving the rook allows 20.♘xg5 – watch out for ♕h5. So Garry decided to ditch the exchange: **19...♘7g6 20.♘xd6 ♕xd6 21.♗g2 g4 22.♗e4 f3 23.♘c2 ♘f7! 24.♖e1?**
'Instead, 24.♗c1, preventing ♘g5, would have been more resilient, but even so 24...♕e7 followed by ...♘d6 would still leave Black in command. At this moment Garry's whole body relaxed – and without looking at the board I knew that the game was as good as over.'

Dan had the advantage of standing behind Kasparov's back: paradoxically this gave him a better read on the ex-World Champion's body language than I could obtain face to face. All I can say is that from this privileged perspective I found him intimidating at every stage of the game. Perhaps this was the one occasion where the medium of radio was inadequate: or at least I as presenter did not have the vocabulary to communicate to listeners the power of the Kasparov glare – and the physical force with which he screws the pieces into the board.

Playing and interviewing the world's strongest woman player, Hou Yifan, was an altogether more relaxing experience – and perhaps she relaxed too much, given what happened at one point in our game. Yifan is a truly delightful person. Her modesty is almost disconcerting – and I was surprised when she answered one of my questions with the observation that in chess women had an inherent disadvantage against men. This was not quite the Nigel Short 'differently wired' version – more that she felt the sheer effort and duration of concentration involved at the highest level required a physical strength that men had more of. In fact, she was unconsciously echoing what Magnus told me in our interview – that he regarded chess as first and foremost a sport, and that he felt it was his better physical condition than Vishy Anand's that lay behind his victory in their first match.

Anyway, while having this conversation with Yifan, we reached the following position.

Hou Yifan-Dominic Lawson

Here, Yifan played **18.f3?** Without really thinking – the talk took up a lot of our half an hour each, so these became more like rapid games – I retreated **18...♘d6?** and was duly squished in 50 moves. Some thought at the board might have revealed that 18...♗h6! is highly embarrassing for White – although afterwards I told a faintly incredulous Dave Edmonds (who thought I was being crushed from first to last) that even if I had found that move, Yifan would certainly have gone on to out-play me.

After the third (and, I fear, final) set of episodes Dan King wrote: 'Looking at his games in this series, I would put Dominic's rating at around 2200 (ECF 200) – and that is a slight drawback: apart from the serious chess players he has been able to dispose of most of his interviewees with ease.' Actually it is a number of years since my classical rating was around the ECF 200 mark. A more likely reason why I was able to dispatch so many of my celebrated non-professional opponents with relative ease is that I had become used to the unusual format of taking part in an interview while playing moves simultaneously. For each of them it was a completely novel experience. Also, as Dan observed, I had 'honed a devilish piece of gamesmanship' by playing challenging moves while asking 'a searching question' at exactly the same moment. One of my earliest opponents, the then Labour shadow Work and Pensions Secretary, Rachel Reeves – a former British girls' chess champion – took exception to this, complaining volubly and repeatedly that it was 'not fair'. She was quite right, of course.

Sir Richard Branson, one of the celebrities that declined to appear on Across the Board, studies a chess position. Going by the way the board and pieces are set up, he may well be on virgin territory.

I would have liked to have lured even more eminent politicians than Rachel into taking part – and tried hardest to convince George Osborne, the Chancellor of the Exchequer, who I knew to be interested in chess (and who I managed to persuade to host a party at 11 Downing Street for the competitors in the London 2013 Candidates' tournament). But George told me that as Chancellor, he was expected to be good at numbers and that as chess is somehow associated with mathematics in the public eye it would do his reputation for fiscal competence no good if he were to lose – as he was certain he would.

So that was one that got away – and there were others: Boris Becker, Freddie Flintoff, Martin Amis and Peter Thiel all ducked the challenge. But, largely thanks to Dave Edmonds's persistence – and of course, the unique pulling power of the BBC – we had some remarkable participants. From the world of physical sport, there were Lennox Lewis, Sol Campbell and Steve Davis – and it was fascinating to see how much the competitiveness that made them leaders in their respective fields of boxing, soccer and snooker was palpable in their determination at the chess board.

I have no idea if the listening public were more interested in chess by the end of the three series – though that was certainly my ambition. But what fun it was to take part. And Gwyneth, you were right: chess somehow matters. ∎

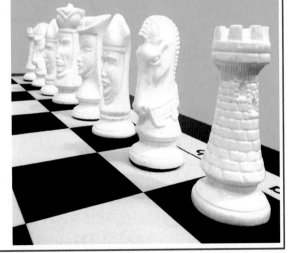

A beaming Levon Aronian receives the Sinquefield Cup from chess benefactors Jeanne and Rex Sinquefield, who were clearly pleased with the winner.

Aronian sweeps America

With a dashing return to good form, Levon Aronian elated his fans and silenced his critics as he claimed the 2015 Sinquefield Cup. The Armenian was never in any danger and beat all three Americans. Magnus Carlsen keeps searching for his old self, but the World Champion is still within striking distance of the overall leader in the Grand Chess Tour, Veselin Topalov.

Dirk Jan ten Geuzendam

Three hotspots in America's chess mecca: the Saint Louis Chess Club, the Kingside Diner and the World Chess Hall of Fame.

R eturning to St. Louis is like gliding into a warm bath, not only because of the sunny weather that welcomes me, but also because the chess microcosmos on Maryland Avenue looks so familiar and inviting. Outside the Saint Louis Chess Club and Scholastic Center, all tables under the trees on the footpath are occupied by blitz players. Through the window I see several staff members dealing with visitors' questions at the front desk. On the opposite side of the street, in front of the World Chess Hall of fame, kids are playing chess, dragging around the pieces of the big outdoor set. Everything looks almost the same as when I left a year ago, until I notice that Lester's, the sports bar next to the Club, has a new name. It's now called Kingside Diner and has a chess king in its logo. Inside, there is more chess, including chess kings and queens pointing at the rest rooms. At the Kingside you can follow the games of the Sinquefield Cup on television screens above the bar, while enjoying the discounted chess menu (50% off normal prices) or have a complimentary soft drink and listen to grandmasters in the commentary room. I am told that in the morning, Rex Sinquefield, who as you may have guessed is the new owner, drops by for breakfast and a chat with grandmasters who prefer the food here to that of

the posh Chase Park Plaza Hotel down the road, where they are staying.

If it's good, it can always be better, seems to be the motto of Rex Sinquefield and his wife Jeanne, who continue to encourage and financially support new initiatives on both sides of the street. The Club is flourishing and hosts tournaments all through the year, including the American junior, the women's and the overall championships. And there always seems to be the ambition to do more. For next year the Club has announced a collaboration with Saint Louis University to establish a chess team that will enter the American collegiate championship at the end of 2016. In the meantime, the head of the team, Alejandro Ramirez, Grandmaster in Residence at the Club, has started recruiting top-tier chess players from around the globe to come to St. Louis, 'reinforcing the image of the city as the mecca of chess'. In the press release no mention is made of the chess team of Webster University, also based in St. Louis, but it seems safe to say that there is a wish to do better than the team led by Susan Polgar and her husband Paul Truong, both of whom are persona non grata at the St. Louis Chess Club.

Opposite the Club, the World Chess Hall of Fame also bustles with activity almost incessantly. Besides a continuous programme of classical concerts and a wide variety of cultural manifestations, it organizes a stunning number of top-class exhibitions related to chess. Within an hour of my arrival I am at a reception of the Chess Collectors International, which has come to St. Louis for one of its annual meetings. Special guest is Jon Crumiller, who possesses arguably

the most important chess set collection in the world. A stunning selection of his finest ivory sets is on display on the first floor. As he explains in a lecture the next day, Crumiller is a staunch advocate of the ban on the trade of ivory, but would like to see a more lenient attitude by the American government towards antique ivory works of art, so that they can be preserved for posterity in museums and other collections. His show is only one of three in the Hall of Fame during the Sinquefield Cup. On the second floor the exhibition 'Battle on the Board' tells the story of the role chess played in the Second World War, while on the ground floor there are works of art by Canadian artist Marcel Dzama that were inspired by notable predecessors such as Marcel Duchamp, Man Ray and Yoko Ono.

The wish to improve and expand was also reflected in the third Sinquefield Cup. Following the double-round robins in 2013 and 2014 with four and six players, the 2015 edition was a 10-player all-play-all that doubled as the second leg of the Grand Chess Tour. Apart from the number of players, the main difference with the previous events was perhaps the huge van behind the club crammed with high-tech gadgetry that served as the production room for the top-notch live broadcasts. The van was custom-built for the television company of Rex Sinquefield's son Randy and will be used to broadcast major sports events as well.

After his shocking performance in the first leg of the Tour, Norway Chess, where he lost four games, Magnus Carlsen was doubtlessly motivated to show his best, especially since he was not too happy either that he had played second fiddle in St. Louis last year, when Fabiano Caruana won his first seven games and finished three points ahead of the World Champion. As Carlsen put it at the opening ceremony, last year he had been a spectator, this time he wanted to take part. But in Round 1 he immediately got a cold shower. As in Stavanger, he played against Veselin Topalov, and again he lost, albeit this time not on time in a winning position. Confronted by an early opening novelty, Carlsen ambitiously sacrificed a piece and remained ambitious when it had become high time to start looking for drawing chances.

When Topalov also won his second game, a fine strategic effort against Hikaru Nakamura, speculation was rife that the winner of Norway Chess might also claim the second leg of the Grand Chess Tour. That dream went up in smoke in Rounds 5 and 6. First the Bulgarian was punished for his fighting spirit when he courageously sidestepped a move repetition against Fabiano Caruana, and then, in the

next round, Maxime Vachier-Lagrave craftily blew up his Berlin Wall.

In the end Topalov scored 50 per cent and finished shared 6th with Alexander Grischuk, but he still maintained his top place in the Grand Chess Tour standings. As always, he was careful not to get carried away and evaluated his performance in a sober manner: 'It was a dream start, but then I ran out of energy, which in a way is logical. When you play nine tough games, it is impossible to play all these games at the same high level. You always have one bad day. In the past, the players would make a quick draw, but this is no longer an option. And I am the second oldest. It's not like I am completely gone, but I am playing guys that are 20 years younger. Of course I could not have expected a couple of months ago that I would be leading in the Grand Chess Tour, but it doesn't mean very

> **Veselin Topalov: 'I believe that in Norway people should realize that Magnus is facing very tough opposition.'**

much. It could help me to finish second or third in the overall standings, but not to win. The only way to win the Grand Chess Tour is to win in London, in December. I don't think second place will work, because the probability that Magnus or Hikaru or Levon will win is quite high, and then they would always overtake me by one or two points.'

Topalov's win against Carlsen was not the only echo of Stavanger in the first round. As in Norway, Anish Giri met Alexander Grischuk and again he won. It was the Dutchman's only win in St. Louis, but he didn't lose any games either. Against Aronian he was in deep trouble, but he drew that game, too, and after two tournaments, Giri is the only unbeaten player. Thanks to his recent stability, Giri will most likely qualify for the Candidates' tournament next March on rating, just like Topalov.

Carlsen did win his second game, but needed a helping hand from Caruana. In a crazy time-scramble, with both players down to seconds and the position about equal, Caruana blitzed out his 40th move, a blunder that lost on the spot. This was a lucky break for Carlsen, but good wins against Vachier-Lagrave and So seemed to underline that he was fighting for first place, until he spoiled at least one full point in Rounds 7 and 8. First he let an advantage slip and then went on to lose against Grischuk. The next day, in 'a moment of insanity' he threw away a winning advantage against Nakamura and had to settle for a draw. In the end, Carlsen finished on plus-1, just like Nakamura, Vachier-Lagrave and Giri, but thanks to the Grand Tour tiebreaker the Norwe-

Fabiano Caruana was only a shadow of the tornado who won his first seven games last year, but obviously the returned American remained a welcome victim for selfies.

gian was awarded second place, leaving him within striking distance of leader Topalov in the overall standings. Still, Carlsen was sorely disappointed and struggled to conceal his frustration after the second leg of the Grand Chess Tour had not brought him what he had been hoping for.

In Stavanger, Topalov tried to explain that it is not a miracle that Carlsen loses games. In St. Louis he added a similar observation that in any case offers food for thought: 'I think the expectations for him are too high. With the computers we are all almost equal in the beginning and then you have a margin of like 20 moves when you have to make the difference. But he is playing against very strong opponents and I believe it is good that he is losing these games. People realize that he is not the only one and that there are also other fantastic players. It reminds me of these long matches between Karpov and Kasparov; they were taking months. And people kind of believed that these two guys were the real geniuses and that the rest could hardly move the pieces. That's completely untrue. I believe that in Norway people should realize that he is facing very tough opposition. Of course his last two tournaments are way below his level, but these things happen.'

Fabiano Caruana faced a thankless task in St. Louis after his stellar performance last year, but losing his first two games, against Aronian and Carlsen, must have taken its toll. He finished on minus-2 and dropped 11.9 rating points. Caruana arrived with a new second, Rustam Kasimdzhanov, who replaced Vladimir Chuchelov, the man with whom he had been so successful, and his new manager Lawrence Trent. On his way to St. Louis, Trent tweeted jokingly: no pressure @FabianoCaruana, but I expect a much better performance this year ☺.

In the end it was probably the manager who got more publicity than his

ward, when late at night after the last round he lost a $1,000 bet against Magnus Carlsen during a memorable evening full of blitz and trash talk at the Club. Trent (IM, 2452) had bet that of 10 blitz games he would not lose four if Carlsen gave rook odds. This proved a risky bet. Trent won five of the first eight games, but the room exploded when in the 9th game the World Champion won his fourth game despite the handicap of a full rook!

For the first time, Caruana, Nakamura and So, the pillars of the new American Dream Team, played together in one tournament representing the US. Wesley So fared even worse than Caruana, and finished in bottom place. Three losses in a row in Rounds 4 to 6 rocked his self-confidence, but did not affect his sense of humour when he commented: 'It's a chess university for me and I am paying with my rating points.' Thirteen points, to be precise. So didn't look for excuses, but he was nervous when he arrived in St. Louis. Fearing that there might be incidents like last year, when his natural mother and

an aunt came to the tournament and harassed him, he had asked his new family to come with him and be in St. Louis from the beginning till the end.

One of Wesley So's losses was against Hikaru Nakamura, in the latter's pet King's Indian.

So-Nakamura
St. Louis 2015 (6)
position after 24.♗e1

White had played the opening very quickly, but while directing his pieces to the queenside, Black built up a dream KID on the kingside. **24... h4 25.fxg4 f3! 26.gxf3 ♘xe4! 27.♖d1 ♖xf3! 28.♖xd7 ♖f1+ 29.♔g2 ♗e3**

Hikaru Nakamura remained combative till the very last day, when a win against against Grischuk brought him third place in St. Louis and second place in the overall Grand Chess Tour standings.

A beautiful and artistic move. **30.♗g3** As 30.♗xf1 leads to a quick mate: 30...h3+ 31.♔xh3 ♘g5+ 32.♔g3 ♕f3 mate. **30...hxg3 31.♖xf1 ♘h4+ 32.♔h3 ♕h6**

The white king is caught in a mating net. So chivalrously allows himself to be mated. **33.g5 ♘xg5+ 34.♔g4 ♘hf3 35.♘f2 ♕h4+ 36.♔f5 ♖f8+ 37.♔g6 ♖f6+** Nice. **38.♔xf6 ♘e4+ 39.♔g6 ♕g5**

Mate.

Nakamura remained combative and eager till the very last day, when he ground down Grischuk in a long fight and secured third place in St. Louis and second place in the overall standings, only one point behind Topalov.

But the hero of St. Louis was the player who beat all three Americans and was never in any danger in the remaining games. Playing creative and strong chess, Levon Aronian won his first super-tournament since Wijk aan Zee 2014. For our games section the winner annotated his win against So ('Sacrificing a piece against Wesley was a great joy') and in an exclusive interview he speaks about his comeback and discloses the changes in his new approach to chess. When the interview was done and I had switched off the tape-recorder, I asked, as an afterthought: 'How relieved are you?' And he replied: 'I wouldn't say that I am relieved. But I can say that I am satisfied. That would be the word. I wasn't really sitting there, moaning, ah, things have not gone right. I knew that at some point I would do what I did.'

NOTES BY
Levon Aronian

NI 30.1 – E20
Wesley So
Levon Aronian
St. Louis 2015

1.d4 ♘f6 2.c4 e6 3.♘c3 ♗b4 4.f3

I think that Wesley's decision to go in for one of the sharpest variations of the Nimzo-Indian Defence was based on our previous meeting (Wijk aan Zee 2015), where in a sharp position, favourable for me, I blundered a piece.

4...c5 I had not played this before, but I remembered something about it. After this move the game transposes into a Benoni with the bishop on b4, in which every half tempo acquires enormous importance. **5.d5 0-0 6.e4 d6**

The most fashionable move is 6...b5, but I prefer a solid set-up. The position after 6...d6 is very interesting. The main intrigue is whether or not White will succeed unhindered in castling kingside, leaving the black bishops looking silly. Black cannot allow White to develop his pieces and leave the centre untouched, since in this case, because of the absence of his bishop from the lawful g7-square, he will most probably be mated.

7.♘e2 Ten years ago I won an important game in the European Championship against Efimenko after 7.♗d2 exd5 8.cxd5 ♘h5 9.g4 ♕h4+ 10.♔e2 ♘g3+ 11.hxg3 ♕xh1 12.♔f2. The game developed in an uneven and interesting fashion.

7...a6 A very rare move, the chief aim of which is to unhurriedly carry out the thematic ...b5.

8.a4

Instead of this move White has a mass of interesting possibilities, including ♘f4, ♘g3 and even the exotic h4. The move in the game appears to put a stop to the idea of ...b5, but the situation proves to be more complicated.

8...♗a5

A move of which the author of this entire variation, my friend Peter Leko, is very proud. Now, exploiting the advantageous blocking of the a-file, Black is threatening to play ...b5. On seeing this move for the first time, I was so inspired that I employed a similar idea in a game with Anand (Alekhine Memorial 2013).

9.♗d2 I no longer remembered how to play after this move, but on this occasion too I was helped by belief in my talent. As one of my favourite opponents, Hikaru N., once aptly said: 'Form is temporary but class, class is permanent.' Precisely!

9...exd5 10.cxd5

It is clear that both 10.♘xd5 and 10.exd5 are anti-positional. After the former Black can play as he pleases (10...♘c6 or 10...♘xd5 11.cxd5 f5), while after 10.exd5 ♖e8, White has problems with his development.

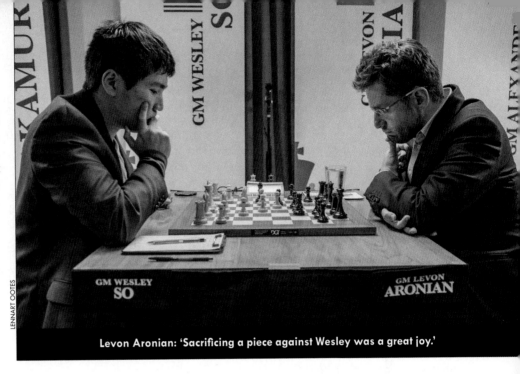

Levon Aronian: 'Sacrificing a piece against Wesley was a great joy.'

10...♘h5

An important move. I had no desire at all to allow White to develop unhindered with 11.♘g3. Now this is met by the highly unpleasant 11...♕h4.

11.g3

The only sensible move. When playing ...♘h5 I initially studied 11.h4. After 11...♘d7 12.g4 ♘e5 13.♗g2, apart from the simple 13...♘d3+ 14.♔f1 ♘f6, with an excellent position thanks to the knight on d3 and threats of capturing on g4, Black also has 13...♗xg4 14.fxg4 ♘d3+ 15.♔f1 ♕f6+, with an attack.

It should be mentioned that after the mysterious computer recommendation 11.♕c1, Black at the least has 11...f5 12.exf5 ♖xf5 with the advantage.

11...♘d7

Very often in similar situations Black plays ...f5, but I had another, more aggressive idea.

12.♗g2 b5

A timely move, since with the bishop on f1, after ...b5 White could have had additional ideas such as axb5 axb5 ♘c1. But now the bishop on g2 is a spectator.

13.g4

The critical move. After 13.0-0 b4 14.♘b1 (on a2 the knight has altogether no prospects) 14...♗b6 with the idea of ...a5 and ...♗a6 (in order not to allow the b1-knight to go to c4) Black has a very pleasant position.

13...b4

A conservative choice, but after 13...♕h4+ I did not like 14.♘g3 ♘xg3 15.hxg3 ♕xg3+ 16.♔f1, with compensation and chances of an attack for White, and I certainly did not want to retreat. Very often in complicated positions it is more important to have the initiative, rather than a possible advantage.

14.♘b1 A mistake, after which it is not apparent how White can save himself. During the game I thought that after 14.gxh5 bxc3 15.bxc3 ♕h4+ 16.♘g3 ♘e5 17.0-0 f5 my position was slightly more pleasant, but analysis shows that after 18.exf5 ♗xf5 19.♘xf5 ♖xf5 20.f4 ♘d3 21.♕e2 White has sufficient resources for maintaining the dynamic balance. Black may be able to fight for an advantage with 17...♖b8, but in any case White has no reason to despair. Now, however, Black's attack cannot be halted.

14...♕h4+ 15.♔f1 With the knight on b1 it is hard to believe in ♘g3.
15...♘e5 I think that Wesley underestimated this sacrifice, and he rightly thought that after 15...♘hf6 16.♗f4 he would have a perfectly good game, since White quickly plays his knight from b1 to c4.

16.♗e1
After thinking for a long time my opponent chose the most natural move. In the event of 16.gxh5 f5 Black's attack looks frightening.

> 'Very often in complicated positions it is more important to have the initiative, rather than a possible advantage.'

16...♕f6 The natural 16...♕e7 did not appeal to me because of the solid 17.♘d2, when, although I have a good position after 17...♘f6, there is no direct punishment. The move in the game maintains Black's initiative.
17.gxh5 ♘xf3 18.♗f2 ♗g4
A continuation of the practical strategy. I realized that after 18...♕xb2 19.♗xf3 ♕xa1 20.♔g2 f5 I was most probably better, but I did not want to take my foot off the gas.

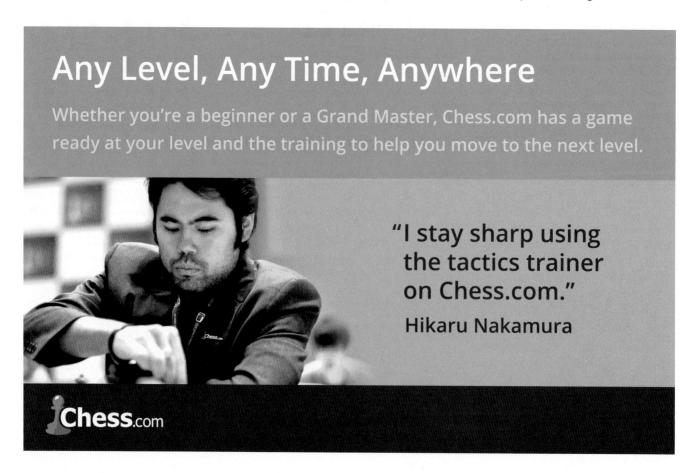

19.♕c1 This mistake leads to a rapid rout, but also after the better 19.h3 ♗xh5 20.♘d2 ♘d4 21.e5 ♕xe5 22.♗xd4 cxd4, with material roughly equal, Black's attack is bound to lead to a win.

19...♘d4 The simplest. The other tempting move, 19...♘e5, did not appeal to me so much, since I could not see a forced win there.

20.♘xd4

Because of the threatened fork 20...♘b3, White has no choice, but this means that the c-file will come under the command of the black rooks.

20...cxd4 21.e5 After 21.♘d2 ♖ac8 22.♕b1 d3 23.♕xd3 ♕xb2 24.♗d4 ♖c3 great loss of material for White is inevitable.

21...dxe5

Both 21...♕xe5 and 21...♕f5 would also have won, but after seeing the idea with 26...♗f5 I decided not to complicate matters unnecessarily.

22.♘d2 ♖ac8 23.♕b1 23...b3

The final subtlety. The knight is removed from its defensive position.

24.♘xb3 ♗b6

It is not possible to defend against the threats of ...♖c2 and ...d3.

25.a5

25...♗a7 It would be stupid to chase after the queen by 25...♖c2, when there is a simple plan.

26.♔g1 ♗f5

27.♗e4

On seeing that 27.♕e1 and 27.♕f1 are met by the deadly ...e4 followed by ...e3 and ...♖c2, my opponent decided to terminate his suffering.

27...♕g5+ 28.♔f1 ♕f4

After 29.♗xf5 d3 30.♗xh7+ ♔h8 31.♕e1 ♖c2 mate is not far off. For this reason Wesley resigned.

The greatest praise of this game came in a letter from Peter Leko. 'The game was truly in the spirit of ...a6, ...♗a5 as I have imagined! Bravo Maestro!' Thank you Peter! Like valuable wines, your ideas await their turn!

NOTES BY

Veselin Topalov

SI 1.3 – B51
**Magnus Carlsen
Veselin Topalov**
St. Louis 2015 (1)

1.e4 This was not the move I had expected. I generally failed to guess the opening moves of my opponents in this tournament, except maybe for the final round against Aronian and against Caruana.

1...c5 2.♘f3 d6 3.♗b5+ ♘d7 4.0-0

I had already played this before, as had Magnus in a rapid game against Nakamura in Zurich in 2014.

4...♘f6 5.♖e1 a6 6.♗d3 b5 7.c4

Now, if Black takes – 7...bxc4 8.♗xc4 – the bishop is well placed on c4 and White's next move is d4.

7...g5 Nakamura went 7...♘e5. I got the idea for the text-move in early 2014, when one of my seconds, whose name I prefer not to mention, gave me a file. At the time I didn't think I would ever have the opportunity to play it, so I didn't check it at all before the game. After I had played it, Carlsen began to think and there were a lot of people watching who started to like the position. I knew from my file that the line was quite complicated, but I didn't remember whether it was fine for Black or dubious.

8.♘xg5 Sitting at the board and thinking about the position, I believed this was the strongest move. After 8.cxb5 g4 9.♘h4, Black has good compensation and the knight on h4 is in trouble, which is why I believe that White has to play 9.e5, and after 9...dxe5 10.♘g5 it's another story.

8...♘e5 The logical move. And about the only thing I remembered.

9.♗e2
This is better than 9.♗f1 bxc4 10.♘c3, when after 10...h6 11.♘f3 Black has 11...♗g4 and is fine.

9...bxc4

10.♘a3
This looked a bit strange to me. The logical move was 10.d3, when after 10...cxd3 11.♗xd3 White would have a lead in development. But it's a game. I was also looking at 10.f4 ♘d3 11.♗h5 (or 11.♕a4+ ♕d7 12.♕xc4 ♘xe1 13.♕xf7+, which doesn't pose Black any problems either) 11...♘xh5 12.♕xh5 ♘xe1 13.♕xf7+ (13.♘xf7 ♗g4 14.♕xg4 ♔xf7 is barely an improvement, as there is no perpetual) 13...♔d7, and I could not see any problem for Black. There is not even a perpetual check.

10...♖g8
I could also jump 10...♘d3 here, but the move I played appealed to me more.

11.♘xc4
I had considered this move, but it didn't worry me and I was surprised when he played it.

11...♘xc4 12.d4
Played very quickly. This looks interesting, but my impression was that Black has to be OK. I was only not sure whether it was also better for me.

12...♘b6 13.♗h5
During the game I believed it was his intention to play 13.dxc5 dxc5 14.♕xd8+ ♔xd8 15.♘xf7+ ♔e8 16.♘e5, which I assessed as better for Black. But with two pawns for the piece and some positional compensation White might draw. But apparently he decided on 13.♗h5 and sacrificed the piece.

13...♘xh5 14.♕xh5

14...♖g7

For a moment I also considered 14...♖xg5 15.♗xg5 cxd4 16.♕xh7, when White's idea is to go ♕h8 and ♗h6, and Black has to play 16...f6. I believed that Black was fine, but I didn't want to give him all these checks and development, and sometimes the h-pawn can become dangerous.

After the game, when I went to the commentary room, I was told that another nice move was 14...♖g6, which is not a very human move, and only if White takes on h7 – 15.♕xh7 – then 15...♖g7 16.♕h8 cxd4 17.♘h7 ♖xh7 18.♕xh7, and with the bishop on c1 instead of on g5, Black has 18...e5, which would be a better position with two pieces, a strong pawn centre and good coordination for one rook.

15.♘xh7
I had expected 15.dxc5.

15...♕d7
This move I had foreseen and I thought it was a great move, so I played it very quickly. Later the computer claimed that 15...♘d7 was better, but I like to develop my pieces and not go back.

16.dxc5 dxc5

With only the **London Chess Classic** to go, **Veselin Topalov** continues to lead in the overall standings of the Grand Chess Tour.

17.e5
This was a mistake. Instead, 17.♘xf8 was probably about equal, but he had missed 17...♕h3, when after 18.♕xh3 ♗xh3 19.g3 I thought I would at least have a draw. For instance, after 19...♖g8 (after the game I was told that the most precise move was 19...♖c8, protecting the pawn, with the idea to go ...♖c6, to stop the bishop from coming to h6)

ANALYSIS DIAGRAM

20.♗h6 I can start attacking the bishop (but I had missed 20.♘h7 f6 21.e5 ♖h8, when I win a piece, although after 22.♘xf6+ exf6 23.exf6+ ♔f7 it's about equal, because White has many pawns) 20...♖h8 21.♗g7 ♖g8 22.♗h6. But instead of attacking the bishop with ...♖g8 and ...♖h8, my intention was 20...♘c4 21.♖ac1 ♘e5, threatening

check and ...♘g4, winning a piece, which should be a bit better for me. But here I had missed 21.♖ec1 ♘e5 22.♖xc5 ♘g4 23.♖h5, which is very good for White.

17...♕c6
I spent a lot of time before playing this move, although I had seen it immediately.

For some reason I also considered moves like 17...♕e6, but to be honest I no longer remember why it took me so long to finally play 17...♕c6, which is so obvious.

18.f3 This is a bit slow and allows me to swap the queens. I thought he had intended to play 18.♘f6+ ♔d8 19.♘e4, when I can try to swap the queens or go 19...♗b7. I don't recall what I was planning to play. Around here I stopped trying to guess his moves.

18...♕g6 19.♘f6+ ♚d8

20.♕xg6

After 20.♖d1+ I can play both 20...♗d7 and 20...♘d7, but not 20...♚c7, of course, in view of 21.♘e8+.

20...♖xg6 21.♘e4

Anish Giri and his wife Sopiko arrive at the Saint Louis Chess Club. The Dutchman is the only participant in the Grand Chess Tour who has not lost a single game.

He has gone for the position I mentioned before, but now with the queens gone, which he apparently thought was a better version. But it is clear that Black is fine. The only question was how large my advantage was.

21...♗b7 22.h4 As 22.♘xc5 is not good because of 22...♗xf3.

22...♖c8 A natural move, defending the c-pawn.

23.h5

23...♖g8

Here I still thought that White had good chances of making a draw, because sometimes he can put his pawn on g4 and his king on f2 and then wait while the bishop on f8 is closed in. He has two pawns for the piece and might win another one.

But we were both getting low on time.

24.♗d2 Threatening 25.♗a5.

24...♘c4

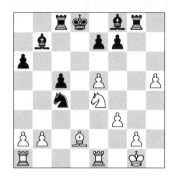

25.♗c3

Protecting the pawn on e5 and intending to play b3. But it allows my bishop to come out. After the game Magnus told me that 25.♖ad1 was a nice trick, as after 25...♘xd2 26.♖xd2+ Black cannot play 26...♚e8, as 27.♘f6+ wins for White. But after 26...♚c7 27.♘xc5 ♗xf3 28.♘xa6+ ♚b6 Black is better.

25...♗h6

26.♖ad1+ This is a clear mistake. He should have played 26.♔f2, when after 26...♔e8 27.g3, I don't have 27...♗f4. Black is fine, of course, but it would have been much better than what he did.

26...♔e8

27.♖d3

The big difference is that here 27.♔f2 loses to 27...♗e3+ 28.♖xe3 ♖xg2+.

27...♗f4 Now the attack on the e5-pawn gives Black a huge advantage. Black is very close to winning. White wants to put his knight on g4 to protect the pawn on e5 and to close the g-file, but it is just a matter of time before Black wins.

28.♘f2 I had expected 28.e6, when I would have to choose between 28...f5

and 28...fxe6, both of which are good for Black.

28...♗c6 A good move, preparing either ...♗b5 or ...♗d7.

29.♘h3

More natural seemed 29.♘g4, when White might have tricks with ♘f6+ or h6. After the text-move I thought I was as good as completely winning.

29...♗g3 30.♖e2 ♗b5

Quickly x-raying the white rooks.

31.♖d1 ♗c6 In time-trouble I noticed I couldn't achieve anything against the rook and quickly withdrew the bishop again.

32.♘f2

Now again the best White can hope for is going to g4. But now Black has a winning tactic.

32...♗xe5 33.♘g4

Since after 33.♖xe5 ♘xe5 34.♗xe5 ♗xf3, followed by ...♖xg2+, Black will be a pawn and an exchange up, as the pawn on h5 will also drop soon.

33...♗xc3 34.bxc3 ♔f8

Sidestepping the check on f6.

35.♔f2 ♖h8

Provoking the h-pawn in order to collect it.

36.♘e5

36...♘xe5

I also considered 36...♗a4 37.♘d7+ ♗xd7 38.♖xd7, when I can take the pawn on h5 or play 38...e6.

37.♖xe5 ♗e8 Defending the pawn on c5.

38.g4 f6 39.♖e6 ♗b5 With a piece for a pawn, Black is completely winning.

40.♖de1 The last attacking move.

40...♖c7

Here I thought he was going to play a bit more, but to my surprise he resigned immediately.

It was a great event and Levon Aronian was the deserved winner, not only because he scored more points than the rest, but also because he never was in any trouble, which made it a very clean victory.

NOTES BY
Alexander Grischuk

SI 11.2 – B92
Magnus Carlsen
Alexander Grischuk
St. Louis 2015 (7)

For some reason I always enjoy playing against Magnus, even though the games usually don't turn out to be very enjoyable for me. This one, however, was an exception.
1.e4 c5 2.♘f3 d6 3.d4 cxd4 4.♘xd4 ♘f6 5.♘c3 a6 6.♗e2 e5 7.♘b3 ♗e7 8.♗e3 ♗e6 9.♕d3 ♘bd7 10.♘d5 0-0 11.0-0

Historically speaking, this position used to be reached via the 9.0-0 0-0 10.♘d5 ♘bd7 11.♕d3 move order, but recently White players have started playing ♕d3 on the 9th or even the 8th move. I am not sure if there is a hidden point behind those finesses or whether it is simply the computer that likes ♕d3 at every opportunity. I guess I should have a look at it one day.
11...♗xd5 12.exd5

> 'I must have some childhood trauma or something', otherwise it is hard to explain why I kept avoiding ...f7-f5 at all cost.'

12...♖c8 The whole line got a boost in popularity after Black rather surprisingly started to have headaches after 12...♘c5 13.♘xc5 (White almost exclusively and not very successfully used to play 13.♕d2) 13...dxc5 14.c4. However, 12...♘c5 is far from being forced.
13.c4 ♘e8
Preparing ...f7-f5, ...g6/...♘g7 or ...♗g5.
14.♕d2 b6

Preventing ♘a5. Now Carlsen starts the standard plan for these positions: ♘a1-c2-a3 (b4). Or so I thought...
15.♖ac1 a5 16.♘a1 g6 17.b4!?

Surprise! As said I only considered 17.♘c2, which actually was no weaker than the text-move.
17...♘g7 The point of 17.b4 is, of course, that after 17...axb4 18.♘c2, the white knight inevitably goes to b4 and then to c6, although the position remains very complicated after 18...f5.
18.bxa5

18...bxa5
When playing 17...♘g7, I had planned 18...♘f5, but here I realized that after 19.♗xb6 ♘xb6 20.axb6 ♗g5 (20...♕xb6 21.♗g4) 21.♕b4, Black may end up in trouble.
19.♗d3
Obviously, after 19.♘b3 ♘f5 20.♘xa5 ♘xe3 21.fxe3 ♗g5 22.♘c6 ♕b6 23.♖c3 ♖a8, Black has fantastic compensation for the pawn.

19...♘c5?!
It was already fine to play ...f7-f5 on either move 16 or 17, but now it was high time for it.
After 19...f5, Black takes over the initiative: 20.f3 (20.f4?! ♘h5! 21.g3 ♘hf6) 20...♘h4! 21.♘b3 f4 22.♗f2 ♗xf2+ 23.♖xf2 ♖a8.
20.♗c2?!

The computer recommends 20.♗xc5, but it looks so ugly that I am not going to analyse it.

However, stronger was 20.♖b1 ♘xd3 21.♕xd3, and I slightly prefer White.

20...a4?!

Again it was better to play 20...f5, and only in case of 21.f3 (the point is that 21.♘b3 loses the bishop: 21...♘xb3 22.♗xb3 f4 23.♗a7 ♕c7) 21...a4.

21.♖b1 Finally one good move from one of us for a change.

21...e4?

My maniacal desire to avoid ...f7-f5 could have cost me dearly. It was not as strong now as on the two previous moves, however, as 21...f5 22.♖b4 leads to very unclear play.

22.♗xc5 ♖xc5 23.♗xa4?

Magnus probably didn't like that after 23.♕e2 f5 24.♗xa4 ♘h5 Black seems to get a kingside attack, but that is an illusion. After 25.♘b3 ♘f4 26.♕c2 ♖c8 27.♘d4, White is in full control and far better.

23...♖xc4 24.♗c6

24...♘f5? I must have some child-hood trauma or something, otherwise it is hard to explain why I kept avoiding ...f7-f5 at all cost. After 24...

As arbiter Chris Bird collects the scoresheets and Alexander Grischuk suggests a move, Magnus Carlsen has self-reproach and utter disgust with his play written all over his face.

f5 25.a4 f4 (or even 25...♗f6 26.a5 ♗e5) Black is absolutely no worse.

But even if I could not overcome my paranoia about ...f7-f5, it was much better to play 24...♗f6 25.♕e2 ♖c3 26.♕xe4 ♖a3 27.♕c4 ♕a5 28.♘b3 ♕a7, and a draw will soon be agreed. The difference between this line and the game will be seen very soon.

25.♕e2 ♖c3 26.♕xe4 ♖a3

27.♕e2?

Letting the advantage slip. After 27.♕c4 ♗f6 (the thing is that after 27...♕a5 White has 28.♗d7!, and Black is in real trouble: 28...♗g7 29.♘c2 ♖c3 – 29...♖xa2? 30.♘b4 ♖a3 31.♘c6 – 30.♕b4) 28.♘c2 ♖c3

29.♕a4 ♗e5 Black has decent drawing chances, but he will have to defend for a long time.

27...♗f6 28.♘b3 ♕e7

Now it is just equal. It is even White who needs to be slightly careful.

29.♕xe7 ♘xe7 30.♘d2 ♖xa2 31.♘c4 ♖d8

32.g4?

Correct was 32.♖fd1 ♘f5 33.g3 ♗d4 34.♖d2. White's position looks slightly dangerous, but in fact Black will never be able to activate his d8-rook, since White controls the a8-, b8- and e8-squares. Thus it should be an easy draw.

32...♗d4

33.♖bd1

I don't want to criticize this move. Magnus had only two minutes here to reach move 40, so his desire to simplify the position is very understandable. Of course, the computer doesn't give up its pawns so easily, and thus recommends 33.♔g2. However, after 33...♚f8 34.♔f3 ♝c5 35.♖a1 ♖xa1 36.♖xa1 ♖b8 it agrees that White will suffer for a long, long time, since 37.♖a8?? ♘xc6 blunders a piece.

33...♝c5 34.♘d2 ♖xd2 35.♘xd2 ♘xc6 36.dxc6 ♖c8 37.♘e4 ♖xc6 38.♖d1

38...h6! To avoid a weakness on h7 after g4-g5.

39.h4 ♚f8 40.♔g2 ♚e7

The time-control has been passed,

and it's time to evaluate the position. I believe that it should be slightly closer to a draw than to a black win, but it is really on the edge and White will have to defend really well to survive.

41.♖c1 After a long think Carlsen decides to defend by pinning the black bishop. However, this approach fails, and eventually Black unpins with some dividends.

Thus it made sense to try 41.h5 or 41.♘c3, aiming for counterplay in some other way.

41...♖c8!

Inaccurate would be 41...♖c7, since after 42.♖e1 ♝d4 (bad is 42...♝b4 43.♖e2 d5? 44.♘c3+ ♚d6?? 45.♘b5+) 43.♘c3+ ♚d7 (43...♝e5 44.♘d5+) 44.♘b5 the rook gets forked.

However, 41...♚e6 was fine as well.

42.♔f3 ♚e6 43.♖c2 ♖c7

44.h5? Now 44.♖e2 is pointless: 44...♝d4 45.♘c3+ ♚e5.

Correct was 44.♘c3! ♖e7 45.♖d2!, and it is very hard for Black to make progress: 45...♖b7 is met by 46.♖e2+ ♚d7 47.♘d5 ♖b3+ 48.♚e4, and I think White should be able to save the game.

44...gxh5 45.gxh5 ♝b6

Now Black should objectively be winning, although the game is very far from over. During the game and before analysing it I was very upset about my play in the next stage, but during analysis I found that it is still very hard for Black to convert his advantage. Apart from that, from this point onward until the rook swap, Magnus defended very well.

46.♖e2 ♝d4 47.♔g3 d5 48.♘d2+ ♚f5 49.♔g2 ♝e5 50.♘f3

50...♝f6

Black should probably win after 50...f6 51.♘h4+ ♚g4 52.♘g6 ♝f4 53.♖e1! ♝d2 54.♖b1 (54.♖d1 ♖c2 55.♘e7 ♝e3) 54...♚xh5 55.♘f8 ♖c2 56.♚f3, but anyway it will not be at all easy.

51.♖a2

51...Rd7 Or 51...d4 52.Ra5+ Ke4 53.Ra6 Bg7 54.Rd6, and it is very hard to push the pawn further.
52.Ne1!

52...Rc7 It is very hard to comment on the next few moves. Both sides have a lot of approximately equal options at almost every turn. I am going to skip ahead a bit. Black could win a pawn with 52...Kg5 53.Nd3 Kxh5 54.Ra5 Kg4 55.Nb4 d4 (55...Kc3 56.Rxd5), but after 56.Nd3 his king is so misplaced that I am not sure if this can be won.
53.Kf3 Bg5 54.Ra5 Ke5 55.Ke2 Ke4 56.Ra4+ d4 57.f3+ Kd5 58.Ra5+ Kc4 59.Nd3 Re7+ 60.Re5

60...Re6?
I had not intended to swap the rooks, of course; I had simply missed 60.Re5 in my calculations. However, it seems that my blunder was extremely unfortunate, since Black is winning after 60...Kc3! 61.Rxe7 Bxe7. There are a lot of lines, but with precise play Black slowly sets up a journey for his king to the h5-pawn: 62.Ne5 Kc2 63.Nd3 Bd6 64.Nf2 Kg3 65.Nd3 Kb3 66.Kd2 Bd6 67.Ke2 Kc4 68.Nb2+ Kd5 69.Nd3 (69.Nd3 Ke6, and the king marches to h5) 69...Bf4 70.Nc4 Be3. Now White has to either let the black king continue his journey or go into a lost pawn ending: 71.Nxe3+ dxe3 72.Kxe3 Ke5 73.f4+ Kd5 (73...Kf5?? 74.Kf3 f6 75.Ke3 Kg4 76.Ke4 Kxh5 77.Kf5) 74.Kd3 f5.

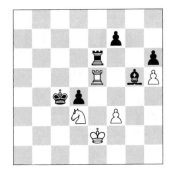

61.f4!
In this position passive play is hopeless. After 61.Rxe6 fxe6 Black puts his pawn on e5 and the bishop on f4,

and then carefully brings his king to the kingside: 62.Nb2+ Kb3 63.Nd3 Kc3 64.Nf2 Bf4 65.Nd3 e5 66.Ne1 Kc4 67.Nd3 Kd5 68.Nb4+ (68.Nf2 Ke6) 68...Ke6 69.Nd3 Kf5 70.Nc6 Kg5 71.Nxd4 exd4 72.Kxd4 Kxh5 73.Kd3 Kh4 74.Ke2 Kg3 75.Kf1 Kh2, and wins.
61...Bf6 62.Rxe6 fxe6

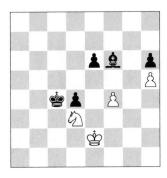

63.Nf2?
The fatal mistake. Instead of withdrawing the knight, White could have saved the game with 63.Kd2, and Black cannot do anything because of the unfortunate position of his bishop: 63...Kd5 (63...Kg7 64.Nb2+ Kd5 65.Kd3; 63...Bd8 64.Ne5+ Kd5 65.Kd3 Bc7 66.Nf3) 64.Ke2 Ke4 65.Nc5+ Kf5 66.Kf3, with a draw.
63...Be7 64.Ng4 Kc3

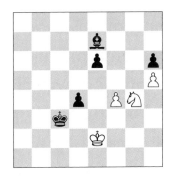

65.f5
White loses because of the zugzwang after 65.Kd1 Bf8 66.Nf2 Kc4 67.Ke2 Bd6 68.Nd3 Kc3.
65...exf5 66.Nxh6 Kc2
The black pawn queens first and so White resigned. ■

'When you're working on your openings, it's as if you're making a suit or a shoe.'

'The world is a better place when Levon Aronian is playing well!' Garry Kasparov's sweet tweet warmly reflected the relief and happiness that the Armenian's fanbase felt after his victory in the Sinquefield Cup. In a frank interview with **Dirk Jan ten Geuzendam,** the winner talks about his changed approach, the role of his fiancée Arianne, the recent results of his good friend Magnus Carlsen, and more.

O n the eve of the Sinquefield Cup, a video circulated online of a swimming contest in a small outside pool. The competitors' speed was seriously hampered by the inflatable animals they were lying on. A voice informed us that the contestants were Magnus Carlsen (on an orca, he won), Peter Heine Nielsen (on a flamingo), and Levon Aronian (on a small air bed). Levon Aronian? What was he doing in a training camp of the World Champion a week before they were to be rivals in the second leg of the Grand Chess Tour? And was it really him? As I peered at the fuzzy footage, I easily

Levon Aronian: 'Normally, in each tournament you have one, two dubious games. Here I didn't have any.'

recognized Carlsen and Nielsen, but I had strong doubts about Aronian. Surely this was a typical Magnus Carlsen prank, trying to create silly rumours and theories. But it was not, as Henrik Carlsen, who also briefly appeared in the video, laughingly told me when I arrived in St. Louis.

As I sit down with Levon Aronian at the end of the Sinquefield Cup to talk about his impressive comeback, he is also amused by my incredulity and lets out his trademark high-pitched laugh when he says: 'But then you saw the swimming and you recognized me!' And he explains how he ended up in a pool with probably his biggest rival while readying himself for a crucial tournament. 'After Norway Chess,

Peter Heine wrote to me, asking if I would care to play some blitz games, do some sports. You know, I compete with Magnus in basketball. So yeah, I was happy to do that and I had the time of my life, really. A great holiday. Being in the Hamptons, next to the sea, was the perfect thing to do before a tournament to physically prepare yourself for long games. We stayed in the house of a friend in South Hampton. We analysed a little bit, things neither of us knew. Played some blitz games, played basketball, we biked, we swam in the ocean, everything.'

He agrees that if you do all those things together, you not only share a passion for chess, but also get along well on a personal level. 'Yeah, we kind of share some things in our personali-

ties, I guess. Deep inside we are very ambitious people. In everything, yes.'

Adjusting to the time difference and acclimatizing seemed a wise thing to do before his third Sinquefield Cup. After all, his first two performances had been huge disappointments. Time and again he had expressed how excited he felt to play in the United States, but both in 2013 and in 2014 his result fell short of his enthusiasm. This time he was confident that he wouldn't let himself down again. After his shared bottom place in Norway Chess he had told himself: 'That's the end of it. This just can't go on.' And his fiancée Arianne had told him the same. They opted for total dedication to achieve his goals. 'You know

I have a really open personality. I like to be with people, I like having dinner with them, but during a tournament it does make it harder for me to concentrate, to cut myself off from everything. After all, I am from the Caucasus, where people get together. Here I went out with others for dinner very little. And I didn't go partying after any games.'

And they stuck to a strict daily routine. 'We woke up around nine. Went to the gym or the pool. Nothing crazy, no heavy exercises, just something to make yourself feel good, then breakfast. Normally I had an hour dedicated to chess, which I think is very healthy. I stopped every chess activity around 12, 12.10. I cut my training one hour before the game (the round started at 13.00 hrs. – DJtG). Had a 15-20 minute nap. Had a shower and went to the game.

'It was good that I arrived here earlier. During the first two days in St. Louis I worked on some of my variations. You need to review your lines before a tournament. That's a good thing to do. Just to plan the whole picture. What you are going to do with each player. I never really had any system for this. It's a new thing for me. I came up with it myself. It's more systematic than what I used to do. I kind of try to structure my general opening approach, the way I am going to play against my opponents. I think it worked. I am happy with the result in general. Normally, in each tournament you have one, two dubious games. Here I didn't have any.

'I felt that things were going well very early on. Actually, immediately after I won my first game (against

> **'I am counting the days till I can play some of the beautiful ideas that I have found.'**

Caruana). It was a very easy game. I didn't really play anything particularly special, but my mindset and the working ethics during the game were good. Of course, I was very upset to spoil that position against Anish (Giri, in Round 3). It was obvious that I had a large advantage after the opening. And the good thing was that it was not obvious to him. The position was really overwhelming, but I just went for the wrong plan. But I think that when Wesley played a very bad game against me the next day, I felt that the tournament was going to be good.'

In the end he won three games and they happened to be against the three Americans – Caruana, So and

A GRANDMASTER AMONG UNIVERSITIES.

If you're interested in playing chess at an American university, we want to hear from you. The University of Texas at Dallas offers highly competitive scholarships to master-level players. For more information, please contact Program Director Jim Stallings at james.stallings@utdallas.edu at least one year in advance of your intended fall enrollment date.

Nakamura – who for the first time played together in a tournament, representing the United Sates. 'Yeah, it looks kind of funny. Because I was really trying to win one more game after these three wins. But Vishy (Anand) played an interesting idea against me, and in the game against Veselin (Topalov, in the last round) I just could not force myself to fight anymore, I just wanted to make a draw. But against Vishy I tried, just for self-respect. Of course if it had been the last round I would not have thought about it at all. And I know that someone like Petrosian and some other guys would just come and make a draw. But that's not what I do. I want to fight and it brings me more joy to have a whole tournament with combative games. Except the one against Vachier, who was too solid.'

The past year was tough for Aronian. The man who had been seen as one of the most likely challengers of Magnus Carlsen even dropped out of the top-10, and speculation was rife that he might have become a has-been. Those who wished him well asked themselves countless times: what's wrong with Levon? What was happening to him, I ask him, and is there good reason to believe that his win in St. Louis is firm proof that we have really seen a change for the better?

'Well, I didn't have time to analyse my mistakes. You know, some things were not working and I didn't really have the time and courage to admit it. Once I admitted it and began to work on it... It's the approach. The way you come to a tournament. You can say, oh, I just want to play or I missed playing, but you don't feel like it. This is something you can trick yourself into thinking. But you should feel it too. You are the first person to feel your own confidence. And I did have the confidence here. I don't think I ever had confidence like this. I know it will be hard to win tournaments, but I am ready. I think I am just a different player now. Yeah, I believe that.'

Levon Aronian and his fiancée Arianne. 'Before she wasn't reading me well, but now she knows me better and understands how to help me better.'

The reactions to his win in the Sinquefield Cup were without exception warm and filled with relief that one of the most creative players of our time had regained the ability to express himself on the chess board. Touching was Garry Kasparov's tweet: The world is a better place when Aronian is playing well! He feels flattered. 'That makes me very happy. Not that I care about what people think of me these days... Of course, it's nice if people are rooting for me. A guy like Garry Kasparov, one of my favourite players, probably my favourite player. I think he knows when he sees a good game. But I've had a year of all kinds of reactions... When you are not confident, those things affect you a lot. But after Norway I didn't care anymore. I had a short talk with Arianne and I told her what I thought I should do, and she told me what she thought and we kind of found a way. That's the right thing to do.'

Levon Aronian and Arianne Caoili have been together since 2006. Earlier this year they got officially engaged. Two years ago, Levon moved back to Yerevan from Berlin, and Arianne

has joined him there. Amongst other things, she is working as a consultant for a government project. At one of the press conferences in St. Louis, he called her his psychologist, and he was not joking. 'No, no. Before she wasn't reading me well, but now she knows me better and understands how to help me better.'

One of the explanations that were proffered for his lacklustre results in the past year was that he had stopped working with some of his former seconds, most notably his good friend Gabriel Sargissian. When I broach the subject, Aronian gives his take on what has happened and provides revealing insights in what he sees as the role of a second and what he hopes to get out of their cooperation.

'Right now, I only work with my second Ashot (Nadanian). Before I used to work a lot with very good friends of mine, who helped me a lot. But you know, the chess opening is something... I don't know, but I think it was Kramnik who said that when you're working on your openings, it's as if you're making a suit or a shoe. You are a shoemaker for yourself. They can make the best shoes in the world, but if they don't fit... So you have to carve those things that you are going to use yourself. Because you understand yourself. And then for the technical part of course you can send it to somebody. But it's really important to make it fit. Certain positions might be fantastic, but I would never play them, because I don't like this type of chess. I didn't really stop working with anybody. There may be big events for which I would of course employ my friends again, but I will keep much more control than ever before.'

While he was going through a difficult patch, the limelight inevitably shone on other players and youngsters who may herald the arrival of a new generation. 'Normally speaking, the generations in chess change every ten years or so. I belong to a really good

LISA!

by GM Jesse Kraai

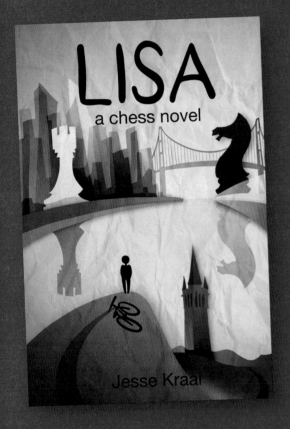

generation, with Grischuk, Ponomariov and Bacrot. But Bacrot and Ponomariov are no longer considered to be elite players. These things happen. Some people collapse and go down. I cannot say that the younger players, like Fabiano (Caruana) or Anish (Giri), are taking over or playing better chess. Not that I don't appreciate what they have achieved. But I just don't see that happening yet. But they have shown, especially Fabiano, that they can play brilliant games.'

Another reason that was regularly given to explain Aronian's disappointing results was the aftereffects of a nose operation that he underwent in early 2014. Whenever any such physical discomfort was mentioned as a possible explanation, he would emphatically state that there was no connection. Yet he had a small flask that looked like a nasal spray next to his board during the Sinquefield Cup. 'Yeah, I do use it occasionally. I mean, it was really good to be next to the sea before the event. Those are the things I need to do every year. That's what my doctor told me. I think it's just a permanent thing, what to do? Going to the sea is not that bad. (With a laugh) If I was told to go to the desert, that would have been ...'

Inevitably we get to talk about the upcoming World Cup in Baku, a complicated issue, as Armenia and Azerbaijan are officially in a state of war. He says he wants to do well and qualify for the Candidates' but acknowledges that it will be difficult. 'Of course there will be mental problems. But you know, it's another test to my system. It will have to stand up to much more than the other players will encounter and feel.'

(As this issue is about to go to press, we know that Aronian didn't succeed in his mission in Baku. In the second round he was knocked out by Ukrainian GM Alexander Areschenko. Not looking for excuses related to the political situation, Aronian blamed his loss on one mistake, a blackout. He praised the excellent organization, which had done everything in their power to make the Armenians feel comfortable – including bodyguards and letting them play their games at the back of the hall to avoid possible provocations from the spectator section. No incidents were reported, but it never could be a completely normal tournament for them. As Aronian noted, nothing really prevented them from going for walks, but they still chose not to leave the hotel.)

As per tradition, I also ask him about his great passion music. I've noticed that he's shifted away from jazz a bit to opera and wonder what he is currently listening to. 'I think it's a natural development. You either go to jazz from classical music or the other way round. And I've been trying to listen to more modern classical music. I'm kind of stuck in the Bruckner era. I just enjoy something schematic and beautiful. Bruckner, Mahler, Hindemith, those are my guys for now.'

This is your eternal hunger for new impressions. Are you equally hungry for more chess?

'Oh, yes, I analyse a lot. I have many ideas I want to play. I am counting the days till I can play some of the beautiful ideas that I have found.'

We started our talk with your good friend Magnus Carlsen and you swimming together in the Hamptons. He seems to have been in a bit of a crisis lately. What's happening to him?

'I don't think there is anything wrong with him. The guy has been winning tournament after tournament and now he didn't win two tournaments in a row. It's like somebody writing nine symphonies and then writing a ballad that is perhaps not so good.'

And you think he will be back to writing symphonies soon?

'Well, I very much hope he won't, because he's my competitor (laughs).'

So you share that too. He also always hopes that his rivals don't do well.

'Yes, but he's a good composer. One of the best.' ∎

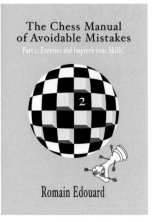

La Guerre psychologique aux échecs: Londres 2013,
Alexander Vuilleumier 268 pages - €26.95, available 10.2015

IM Alexander Vuilleumier was present during
the Candidates Tournament held in London 2013.
He followed the exciting games and tough psychological battles
from the first row. This is Alexander's first book emphasizing
that our game is much more than just playing good moves.
The author provides a precious peek behind the curtains
of this major event.

The Chess Manual of Avoidable Mistakes, part 2
Test yourself and improve!
Romain Edouard 200 pages – €21.95, available 12.2015

One year after his first major publication, Romain Edouard
decided to provide us with even more material enabling the readers
to improve their results in chess. The second volume is packed
with brand new tactical examples and exceptional motifs from
his own games and fellow colleagues. Romain Edouard will steer
you into a disciplined way to improve your skills:
focus and exercise! The book is written in French and English.

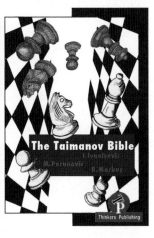

Ivan's Chess Journey Unravelled,
Follow the footsteps of this legendary GM
Ivan Sokolov 275 pages - €28.95, available 12.2015

Ivan Sokolov's was one of the most furious attacking and creative
player of his time.
The author presents an overview of his Life in Chess,
full of entertaining unpublished material. He is not shy to share his
opinions and promises the reader a personal roller coaster loaded
with fun stories and unexpected twists.
We are convinced you will enjoy the ride!

The Taimanov Bible
A complete manual for the Sicilian Player
Ivan Ivanisevic, Milos Perunovic & Robert Markus
450 pages – € 29.95, available 11.2015

The Taimanov has become one of the most popular and complicated
Sicilian variations. Nearly all top players have made good use of this
flexible and positional way of handling this Sicilian. Our Serbian
authors have provided a complete manual with their extensive
'over the board' experience. Their many interesting combative
new ideas tackle the most dangerous and boring lines you may
encounter.
A must read for either player defending the White or Black side.

THINKERS PUBLISHING

Slow Sacrifices

People often associate sacrifices with brilliant mates and forced variations. Those are indeed the most common kinds of sacrifices, but if all variations are forced, it sounds more like an exercise in calculation than a true sacrifice to me. Here, I'd like to talk about sacrifices with which you willingly enter an unknown future, down in material, yet confident about your position. There aren't necessarily any immediate explosions of tactics, but the material imbalance subtly alters the game. As you will see, these sacrifices often depend more on intuition than calculation. But most importantly, it's about a way of thinking.

Mikhail Tal is mostly famous for sacrifices of the explosive kind. Yet, he perfectly captured the essence of the slow sacrifice when he wrote: 'Later, I began to succeed in decisive games. Perhaps because I realized a very simple truth: I was not the only one who was worried; my opponent was worried as well.' Let's start by looking at one such example:

Every player loves to give up material for a devastating attack. **PARIMARJAN NEGI** argues that sacrifices that do not give instant gratification can be even more rewarding.

Black's last move was really asking for ♘d5, especially against Tal, as I am sure Larsen knew. He probably thought he was provoking Tal to make a mistake. After all, despite the nice bishops, the kingside threats don't exactly look lethal.

16.♘d5

Objectively, it's hard to say if this sacrifice is correct – and I wouldn't want to do some long computer analysis to figure that out. Instead, Tal probably noticed that Black can't immediately refute it. There's also a nice aesthetic feel about these two bishops and once Black goes ...g6, there are ideas like h4 and h5. At the same time, it's hard, if not impossible, to reach firm conclusions about the lines after 16...exd5 17.exd5 g6. White has different options, e.g. ♖he1, ♖de1 and h4. But the lines are too complicated to calculate accurately.

16...exd5 17.exd5

Tal-Larsen
Bled 1965 (10)
position after 15...b4

17...f5?

A typical over-reaction of the defender. Here 17...g6 looked like a forced move, but Black probably got overly worried, before calculating anything, by ideas like h4 and h5. So he tries to take more 'drastic' defensive measures.

After 17...g6 18.h4 ♘c5, the computer is very unimpressed by White's chances, probably rightly so. But what does it feel like during a game after a move like ♗c4, which maintains the tension? Also, instead of 18.h4, White could first play ♖de1, with similar ideas. I am certain that Tal did not try to seek an exact solution in these lines, but felt that the tension he had created would be worth it.

18.♖de1

Tal continues to play slowly, maintaining the tension, although objectively 18.gxf6 ♗xf6 19.♕e4 g6 20.♖hg1 might have been stronger. But this involves a lot of forced lines, which would make Black's life much easier. Clearly, it's far more productive to maintain the tension and let Black see ghosts.

18...♖f7?!

Once again, Black sees ghosts and wants to be very safe. 18...♗d8 was a better defensive move, when White has a choice of ideas like h4-h5, etc., or even some snappy ♕h5/♗g7 Stockfish ideas. I would guess that Tal would go for the less forcing idea with h4 etc.

19.h4!
Players often focus on immediate returns after a sacrifice, so Larsen probably considered moves like ♗xf5, etc. But this simple attacking move, threatening g6 and h5, seals his fate, as Black simply isn't ready for this.

19...♗b7 20.♗xf5
A surprising decision. Continuing slowly with 20.h5 seems more in the spirit of the position. I guess Tal had noticed that he would get a large advantage after 20♗xf5 as well, and decided to release the tension.

20...♖xf5 21.♖xe7 ♘e5 22.♕e4 ♕f8 23.fxe5 ♖f4 24.♕e3 ♖f3 25.♕e2 ♕xe7 26.♕xf3 dxe5 27.♖e1 and White converted the advantage without much problems.

My analysis has not been very objective, because this article isn't about the best moves as judged by an omniscient engine. Maybe White has enough compensation, maybe not. But during the game this doesn't matter. It's the psychological aspect that's the most intriguing.

With 16.♘d5, Tal drastically altered the situation, as Black was on his way to completing his development and enjoying a nice and typical Sicilian. After the sacrifice, the onus was on Black to find a defence. The king looked safe on the kingside, but when you look closer, you could see some dangerous ideas. I am sure Tal played it with a cool head and with great confidence. This can make a serious difference in such situations – if you are uncomfortable, this will be noticed. If you spend too much time, or get red ears, or fidget with your pen, or show any other signs of nerves, it really helps to assuage your opponent's doubts. But you need to fuel them!

Nothing about this advice looks hard, but it's not as easy to implement as you'd think.

Here is an example from my own games. I knew I should make the sacrifice, but as I sat there staring at the pieces, I just couldn't do it.

Negi-Sasikiran
Mashhad 2011 (5)
position after 29...♔g7

Of course the ♘f5 sacrifice screams to be played, and I lapsed into a deep think, trying to find a way to finish Black off. But after 20 minutes I had still not found a forced win and in the end I just chickened out and went for a repetition with **30.♗h6+ ♔h8 31.♗g5**

The biggest problem really is the fear. As I noticed during my calculation, after 30.♘f5+ gxf5 31.♗xf5+ ♔h8, White has multiple moves and Black is sort of stuck. I could play 32.♘h6 – forcing 32...♖f8 – when none of the black pieces can move. Or a move like 32.h4, and Black doesn't really have a way to untangle his position. But I couldn't find a killing blow and then the situation – we were playing on the top boards of the Asian Championship – began to play with my mind. What if he defends everything, and I just end up being a piece down? It's hard to pretend that nothing has happened. You're down material! If it goes to an endgame, you will lose. It's so hard to stop thinking about these questions that they shape the way you calculate lines and make you desperate for a quick solution instead of focusing on the challenges your opponent faces. You have to play as if nothing has happened, continue to create and implement plans, look for tactics, stay calm! The endgame is far away, and remember, your sacrifice is playing games with your opponent's mind as well.

This constant urge to keep calculating and find forced solutions might prevent you from seeing the big picture. True, you should start by checking the forced lines – a topic I have touched on before. Even without sacrifices, this helps to give the position a thorough tactical sweep. But once you make sure that it isn't losing, or winning by force, then clinging on to the forced lines can be a mere distraction.

The funny thing is that I wasn't new to the power of the knight on f5:

Negi-Stefansson
Differdange 2008 (6)
position after 20...♘b6

I wasn't particularly happy with my position here. I was a pawn down, and

> 'These sacrifices often depend more on intuition than calculation. But most importantly, it's about a way of thinking.'

just shuffling around the pieces clearly didn't look appealing. Then I saw the idea

21.♘h4!?

with the obvious sacrifice ♘f5 planned next. Clearly, there is no mate on the horizon. It is not even completely clear what White is going to do next. But the knight looks really cool on f5! And I had ideas like ♕f3 and ♕g3 etc. that I felt could give me good compensation. Most importantly, no longer did I feel bored about my position! My opponent, on the other hand, now had to make a big psychological shift: he was probably expecting to play a long, comfortable game. Now he had to deal with an annoying piece sacrifice. There are countless ways to plan for it, but no way to stop the sacrifice. And so the defender started overthinking his options, saw ghosts and went spectacularly wrong:

21...♔f8?! 22.♘hf5 gxf5 23.♘xf5 ♗d8? 24.♕f3

The game has completely changed and the computer shows that White is completely winning, although things didn't feel quite as simple during the game. But the most important thing was that through the next few tense moves I wasn't in a hurry to win, I was willing to continue playing as if it was just another position, that nothing special had happened, and to grab the tactical opportunities when they presented themselves.

24...♘bd7 25.♗c2 ♘c5 26.♗h6+

26.♖ad1 ♘g8 27.♗e3 was winning instantly, but I didn't realize how simple everything was.

26...♔e8 27.♖ad1 ♗e7! 28.♗g5

Allowing Black back in the game, but I

kept my cool and continued with my original plans.

28...♘cd7 29.♕g3 a3 30.♗h4 ♗f8 31.bxa3 ♕xc3

According to the computer my slow play has actually been inaccurate, and Black is better now. But from a practical standpoint, I was able to play my moves relatively quickly and confidently – which is the most important thing with the time running low. The lack of time probably helped me, as there was no time to wonder about what if I don't have enough compensation etc.

32.♗d3 ♖c6 33.♖e3 ♕a5 34.♖f3

Suddenly, a couple of normalish moves, and things have turned around again!

34...d5 35.exd5 ♕xd5 36.♗c2!

Finally, I saw some tactics. Clearly, nothing can be done without seeing some tactics, but as the previous moves showed there is no need to see every possible tactic.

36...♖xc2 37.♖xd5 ♘xd5

A mistake in a bad position, which after **38.♘d6+** leads to mate soon.

One important rule that emerges from this game: You don't have to worry. *You have to continue playing as if nothing has happened.* It's still important to calculate, look for tactics, yet keep track of the positional aesthetics. Improve your pieces. Stop his plans. And most importantly – do not think about what will happen if the sacrifice doesn't work out! Almost no one manages to stay perfectly calm when faced by such a drastic change in the type of position. Players are rattled, they imagine threats, and this often leads to strange decisions that are bound to give you new chances.

But if one doesn't calculate a sacrifice till the end, then how does one decide whether the sacrifice is worth it or not? Aesthetic sense is often a good way to go about it. More specifically, how are your pieces placed? Can you see clear plans to continue improving them?

Kramnik isn't known for his sacrifices, but he has actually played many brilliant games with very intuitive sacrifices.

Kramnik-Fridman
Dortmund 2013 (6)
position after 19...♘d6

Kramnik has been playing very creatively since the opening and here I'm sure that he could not resist an aesthetically pleasing exchange plus pawn sacrifice.

20.f6

He had probably calculated some lines, but more importantly he will have seen how his pieces seem to develop harmoniously (♖f1, ♘f4, ♘h5, ♘c3-jumps, ♕g2 etc.) and the potential of the b2-bishop. Again the most important thing to realize is that, as long as there is not an obvious refutation and your pieces seem to be nice, it's often worth trying it.

20...♗xf6 21.♖xf6 gxf6 22.♘f4 ♘e5 23.♘h5 ♕e7 24.♖f1 ♘d7 25.♕g2!?

The computer prefers the ♕f2-♕f4 plan, but it's far too concrete. Kramnik continues aesthetically and puts his pieces on nice squares. A lot of ideas are hanging in the air. Perhaps not killer blows, but it's really tough being Black when your opponent continues to exert pressure.

25...h6 26.h4

Keeping the tension. The best move according to the computer – ♘e4 – releases the tension easily, and lets Black off the hook.

26...♔f8?!

Black wants to just get out of there of course!

After 26...b5 there are no threats according to the computer. But it doesn't quite look like that when you are staring at this position...

27.♕g3! ♔e8 28.♕f4 ♕f8?

The final mistake. Black should have just given away the h6-pawn. Now, as usual with such sacrifices, Kramnik had to show a sharp mind, to finish it off with **29.♘d5! exd5 30.♗xf6** and it's mate soon!

Black had a lot of options, but nothing that quite relieved the pressure. And Kramnik probably just focused on his nice future plans – bringing the knight to h5, the queen looks pretty and useful on g2, g5 ideas are hanging in the air, etc. In specific lines, it's hard to say if White was creating direct threats or not, but it's so much more exciting to be the one pressing with the initiative than the one waiting for the storm to blow over!

Not all sacrifices are about open kings, of course, although those are admittedly the most interesting. But the general principles of the psychology of such sacrifices are the same. Most importantly, you shouldn't be in a hurry to cash in with forced lines, as keeping the tension often plays games with the mind of your opponent.

Karpov-Kasparov
Moscow 1985 (16)
position after 8.♘a3

This iconic game probably had its roots in Garry's opening lab, but the ideas are still very instructive and in accord with our topic.

8...d5 This doesn't quite seem like a sacrifice, because Black should be able to win the pawn back. But **9.cxd5 exd5 10.exd5 ♘b4 11.♗e2 ♗c5!?**

The key move. Black actually doesn't want to take the pawn back. This is a good moment to pause and try to grasp what is going on. After capturing the d5-pawn, the position will head towards a drawish endgame, with White slightly better developed. This minor edge could become very nasty in the hands of Karpov. Also, White's lousy ♘a3 would probably prove to be quite useful in the endgame because it will have a nice life after moving to c4. Now, when you look closer, you'll notice that the d5-pawn restricts the activity of White's pieces as well – especially if White tries to hang on to it (♘c3, and ♗e2/♗f3, while ♘a3 doesn't have big prospects in the middlegame). On the other hand, none of Black's pieces will have any complaints about the d5-pawn.

12.0-0
12.♗e3! ♗xe3 13.♕a4+ is a nice little tactical trick that should probably promise a slightly better endgame – but Karpov didn't yet feel the need to look for such unusual solutions.

12...0-0 13.♗f3?!
The bishop is just a big dummy on f3, and White probably doesn't yet sense the potential of Black's compensation.

13...♗f5 14.♗g5 ♖e8 15.♕d2?!
Still underestimating Black's compensation. He should bring back the a3-knight into the game, or give away the d5-pawn.

15...b5 16.♖ad1 ♘d3 17.♘ab1
17.d6 and ♘d5, just trying to finally activate the pieces, was still OK. But White stubbornly resists giving the material back.

17...h6 18.♗h4 b4 19.♘a4 ♗d6 20.♗g3 ♖c8 21.b3 g5!?

Kasparov shows no inclination to try to get the pawn back. One thing he makes sure in the next moves is that the b1-knight doesn't get back to the game. White struggled to make any useful moves, and the game did not last long, but the rest is irrelevant for our topic.

So, even the great Karpov completely underestimated Black's compensation, the extra pawn holding him in a seductive grip that he couldn't let go of. While Kasparov focused on just improving his pieces, absolutely ignoring the fact that he was a pawn down.

Conclusion
There is a very fine line between correct and incorrect slow sacrifices. And there is always risk involved – but few of us play for such stakes that losing a game will be the end of the world. If done right, slow sacrifices can add so much more excitement to your game! Once you make sure the immediate tactics do not work against you (is there an obvious tactical refutation?), deciding on a sacrifice is more about attitude. How you feel that day, how does your opponent look? This can all influence your decision. But make sure that the fear of being material down doesn't hold you back. And you don't have to go for every sacrifice you see – but it's already a good start if you at least think about it. ∎

The Power of Love

The tombstone of Vassily Smyslov, who died in 2010 at the age of 89, refers to a painful and tragic episode in the Russian World Champion's life that few people know about. **GENNA SOSONKO** delves into the mystery.

The grave of Vassily Smyslov and his beloved ones in Moscow's Novodevichy Cemetery.

Vassily Vasilievich Smyslov and his wife Nadezhda Andreevna lived happily together for 62 years. They died in advanced old age, not on the same day, but in the same year and just two months apart. On their joint gravestone in Novodevichy Cemetery in Moscow, underneath the words 'Always Together', there is a portrait of the seventh World Champion. Between his and his wife's names, the name Vladimir Selimanov is inscribed. Who was he? Why is he buried with the Smyslovs? And why was his life cut short after just 21 years?

Vassily Vasilievich and Nadezhda Andreevna became husband and wife in 1948. She was three years older than her husband and she already had a son from her first marriage. Very little is known about his father. A few sources quietly muttered that he died in Stalin's purges in the early 1940s. And so Vassily Vasilievich acquired a nine-year old son, and, devoting a great deal of attention to the boy's upbringing, treated him as his own. Not surprisingly, Vladimir was interested in chess, fulfilled the norm for Candidate Master, became one of the strongest juniors in the country, and in 1957, represented the Soviet Union in the World Junior Championship in Toronto.

There is very little information available about this championship. After a long search, and with the

port in Newfoundland, they had to spend 16 hours, but that was only the start of their travel adventures. In the end, after going via New York and Montreal, and arriving a day late, the Soviet delegation made it to Toronto.

After missing his first-round game, Selimanov played Lombardy on the rest day. This ended in a win for the American, who went on to win every game in the tournament – 11 out of 11! 'In a closed Spanish, I played a continuation that I had worked out myself and had tried a couple of times before.

sent the Soviet Union was considered a great honour, and anything less than first place was regarded, if not as a disaster, then at the very least as a failure. The Soviet player was expected to return home only with the gold medal, as 18-year old Boris Spassky had done in the previous World Junior Championship in Antwerp in 1955.

Not very much is known about the subsequent fate of Vladimir Selimanov. He practically did not take part in chess tournaments any further and committed suicide three years later by jumping out of a window. It was said that he made previous attempts to end his life, but had been prevented. One can only imagine what this must have been like for the Smyslovs, especially as they had no other children of their own. Although Smyslov never referred to this tragedy in conversation with me, I am told that to the very end of his life, he would say 'We must go to the cemetery tomorrow, to visit Volodya...'

It was considered that the reason for the young man's suicide was serious psychological problems. Some spoke of schizophrenia, others of suicidomania. I would point out that, in psychiatry, the borderline between 'normal' and 'sick' is blurred and moves constantly. In the Soviet Union, diagnoses of 'schizophrenia' were bandied out rather lightly, although admittedly, in the majority of cases this was in relation to dissidents, who had remained in the country but were fighting the totalitarian regime.

So what really happened? When Smyslov died, Andrew Soltis wrote that his stepson Selimanov was punished after his unsuccessful performance in Toronto and consequently committed suicide. I do not think that Selimanov's problems and suicide (three years later!) were the result of his performance at the World Junior Championship.

In his book *Understanding chess*, Bill Lombardy wrote of the championship: 'Selimanov did not speak English, but language did not prove a barrier for us to get to know each other'.

Toronto 1957. Vladimir Selimanov is standing, extreme left. Standing in the centre is Bill Lombardy (11 out of 11!). Second from right, standing, is Igor Bondarevsky, and on the extreme right, the second to the Philippines representative, Florencio Campomanes, later the President of FIDE (1982-1995).

assistance of the Amsterdam collector Jurgen Stigter, I have managed to unearth a small pamphlet on the tournament in Toronto, with a photograph of the participants.

The account in *Shakhmaty v SSSR* written by Igor Bondarevsky, the young Muscovite's second in Canada, begins with a report of a difficult journey. In Copenhagen, awaiting a connecting flight to Gander, a major air-

The game became sharp, and at the crucial moment, Selimanov missed a tactic', wrote Lombardy.

Second, two full points behind Lombardy, was the German master Mathias Gerusel, third, half a point behind him, the Dutchman Lex Jongsma. And only behind him came Vladimir Selimanov. Eight points out of eleven was not a bad result, but ... only fourth place. The right to repre-

Lombardy was in Toronto with a friend from the Manhattan Chess Club, who spoke Russian, and they often spent time together with Selimanov. Vlad, as they called Vladimir, told them that during the championship he had fallen head over heels in love with a Canadian girl, and that, as soon as he got back to the Soviet Union, he was going to apply for a visa, to return to Canada. Lombardy and his friend categorically advised Selimanov not to return home at all, but to apply for political asylum in Canada.

I would add that the Dutch representative, Lex Jongsma, also remembered a girl of some sort, who came to the tournament several times and watched Selimanov's games. But Lex, not speaking any Russian, 'had no direct contact with the pleasant, but shy Russian'.

The thought of seeing the girl again became an *idée fixe* for Selimanov, especially once it became clear that he could forget about a return visit to Canada. Now nothing else, not even chess, interested him any longer.

I cannot agree with Lombardy, who claims that Selimanov must have said nothing at home of his plans to return to Canada to be with the girl. Since, if he had, Smyslov's contacts could have helped him. I am convinced that even

> **'Lombardy and his friend categorically advised Selimanov not to return home at all.'**

the World Champion, who had won the highest award of all, the Order of Lenin 'for outstanding successes in chess', would have been helpless in this regard. In the Soviet state, there were barriers which nobody could overcome. On the contrary – I am sure that, if they had learned of their son's plans, his parents would have urged him to put any such ideas out of his head. Probably, many parents would do the same, but especially at that time, and in the Soviet Union.

All of this is just speculation, of course, and after half a century it is hard, if not impossible, to establish for sure the reason for the young man's desperate act. We can probably all remember exactly what love is like at the age of 18. Suicide at a young age occurs considerably more often than when older – youth generally has a more carefree attitude to the phenomenon of life than do the fearful elderly.

Was Selimanov's decision influenced, as later claimed, by some mental imbalance? Or was his declining mood brought about by the realisation of the impossibility of achieving what seemed to him to be the only thing that mattered – being with the object of his love? Or was it a combination of these factors? It is as in chess – do you play poorly because you feel bad, or do you feel bad because things are not working out on the board?

What would have happened to Selimanov, if he had followed Bill Lombardy's advice? Would his feelings have withstood the test of time, or would the couple have parted, as often happens with young love? Would he have gone on to university, understanding that professional chess would mean a very hard existence? Or would he have remained in the chess world, as Igor Ivanov did a quarter of a century later?

Would he have got homesick and returned to the Soviet Union? There is no doubt that the Soviet authorities would have done all they could to ensure this, as they did with other defectors, such as Kortchnoi.

There is no answer to these questions. All that we have is a name on a gravestone in Novodevichy Cemetery in Moscow and a small footnote in the history of our game and of that perplexing time. ∎

MAXIMize
your Tactics
with **Maxim Notkin**

Find the best move in the positions below

Solutions on page 105

1. White to move

2. White to move

3. Black to move

4. White to move

5. White to move

6. White to move

7. White to move

8. White to move

9. White to move

Side-stepping the Sicilian ... on move 2!

JEROEN BOSCH

'The bishop move certainly looks silly. At the same time, there is nothing silly about the ratings of Gawain Jones, Vladimir Fedoseev and Igor Kovalenko.'

1.e4 c5 2.♗e2

Recently, some strong grandmasters played this modest-looking bishop move a few times with considerable success. I must confess that I was reminded of Khalifman's reaction when Zviagintsev confronted him with 2.♘a3 at the 2005 Russian Super-Final: he burst out laughing and shook his head in disbelief. It was Zviagintsev, however, who had the last laugh taking the full point home.

Still, even with this outcome in mind, I wouldn't hesitate to state that the bishop move certainly looks silly. At the same time, there is nothing silly about the ratings of Gawain Jones, Vladimir Fedoseev and Igor Kovalenko, all of whom have won games with 2.♗e2 recently.

These grandmasters want to play a particular set-up characterized by the subsequent moves f4, d3, ♘f3, 0-0, c3 and ♕e1. A Grand Prix Attack of sorts, but actually more like a Dutch Defence and then the so-called Ilyin-Zhenevsky Variation with a couple of extras. White being White, he has an extra move, of course, but more importantly he has succeeded in playing both e4 and f4. By comparison, in the Dutch Defence, Black painstakingly aims for ...e6-e5 in the Ilyin-Zhenevsky, which is also the reason why I wouldn't call this the Bird (after 1.f4 the move 1...d5! similarly prevents an early e4). So the modern idea behind 2.♗e2 is to play for this very decent set-up.

Note that 2.f4 d5! would throw a spanner in the works, which is why they play 2.♗e2! – now deserving an exclam for the idea behind the slow bishop move. Perhaps this is not such a Silly Opening Surprise after all, and I propose that we postpone our judgement until we have seen the actual games.

Another very relevant move order is 2.d3, to try and reach a similar position. Some white players then prefer set-ups à la the Closed Sicilian with g3 and ♗g2, but others prefer f4, ♗e2, ♘f3, as in our SOS line. Thus, 2.d3 has a certain flexibility when it comes to how to treat the king's bishop, but 2.♗e2 has a certain advantage too.

A problem after 2.d3 is that 2...d5 3.exd5 ♕xd5 4.♘c3 ♕d8, as successfully played by Bologan as Black, is a serious option after 2.d3.

After 2.♗e2 the 'Scandinavian' is less good:

2...d5 3.exd5 ♕xd5 4.♘f3

This compares favourably, of course, to the position after 2.d3 d5 3.exd5

♕xd5 – White has already developed his king's bishop, which is not hampered by a pawn on d3.

4...♘f6 5.0-0 ♘c6 6.♘a3!?
Turning the position into a kind of favourable 2.c3 Sicilian. 6.♘c3 is playable too.

6...a6 If 6...e6 then 7.d4! cxd4 8.♘b5.
7.♘c4 ♕d8 8.d4!? cxd4 9.c3!

Because Black can hardly take this pawn, Jones manages to transpose to a 2.c3 Sicilian that favours White.
9...e6 Not 9...dxc3? 10.♕xd8+ ♔xd8 11.♘b6! ♖a7 (11...♖b8 12.♗f4) 12.♘g5, with a large advantage.
10.♘xd4 ♘xd4 11.♕xd4!?
Also good is 11.cxd4 ♗e7, and now the annoying 12.♕b3! b5 13.♘e5 ♗b7 (13...♕xd4 14.♗f3; 13...0-0 14.♘c6) 14.♗xb5+!, Al.Karpov-Parkhomenko, Koltsovo 2006.
11...♕xd4 12.cxd4 ♗d7 13.♗f3
because of his pressure on Black's queenside the queenless middlegame favours White, Jones-Madebrink, Lund 2015.

Now that we have seen why 2.♗e2 may compare favourably to 2.d3, it is time to see a few games.

Vladimir Fedoseev
Yu Yangyi
Ningbo 2015

In the 2015 China-Russia match, Vladimir Fedoseev beat Yu Yangyi in what is one of the most natural lines after 2.♗e2.

1.e4 c5 2.♗e2 ♘c6 3.f4 g6
Fianchettoing the bishop is natural and a common remedy against many off-beat Sicilians. Too modest is 3...d6 4.♘f3 ♘f6 5.d3 ♗g4?! (5...g6 transposes to our main game) 6.0-0 e6 7.♘bd2 ♗e7 8.h3 ♗xf3 9.♘xf3, and with two bishops White can be satisfied with the outcome of the opening, A.Greet-Gormally, Hastings 2009/10.
4.♘f3 ♗g7 5.0-0 d6
An important alternative is 5...d5 6.d3, which leads to a position that is often reached via 2.d3. The game may continue 6...♘f6 (6...e6 7.♘a3 ♘ge7 8.c3 0-0 9.♔h1 ♖b8 was Larsen-Kavalek, Bauang 1973 – this game started as a Bird Opening – a serious option was 7.c3 ♘ge7 8.♕e1) 7.e5 ♘g4 (7...♘d7 8.c4! ♘b6 9.♗e3 d4 10.♗f2 f6 11.♗g3 is probably about equal, but fun to play, Jones-Gallagher, Aix-les-Bains 2011) 8.c3 d4 (8...f6 9.d4 ♕b6 10.♔h1 0-0 11.dxc5! ♕xc5 12.♘d4 is better for White, Jones-Palliser, England 2011) 9.♘g5! ♘h6 10.♗f3 dxc3!? (10...0-0 11.♗xc6 bxc6 12.c4 was White's idea) 11.bxc3 ♘d4!? 12.cxd4 (objectively, 12.♗e4 promises a slight edge) 12...♕xd4+ 13.♖f2 ♕xa1 14.♖b2.

This was McShane's idea. Her majesty is under lock and key. 14...♘f5? (14...f6 leads to a draw according to the engines, but finding your way

around these lines is hardly human. Perhaps a kind of inverted Turing test is in the making here?) So far we have followed McShane-Van Wely, London 2009, where White eventually won. Actually, McShane could have won outright with the neat silicon line 15.♗xb7! ♗xb7 16.♕a4+ ♔f8 17.♕b3 c4 18.♕xc4 e6 19.♖xb7 ♘h6 20.♖xf7+ ♔xf7 21.♕xe6 ♘xg5 22.♗a3 mate!

6.d3 ♘f6
Again this is natural, but moving the e-pawn has to be considered, too: 6...e5 7.c3 (7.fxe5) 7...♘ge7 8.fxe5! dxe5 (White is better after 8...♘xe5 9.♘xe5 ♗xe5 – 9...dxe5 loses a pawn to 10.♕a4+! ♗d7 11.♕c4 – 10.♘a3, with the threats of 11.♘c4 and 12.♗f4) 9.♗e3 b6 10.a3! a5 (10...0-0 11.b4) 11.a4 (a common strategic motif: White has gained solid control of the squares b5 and c4) 11...0-0 12.♘a3 h6 13.♕e1 ♗e6? 14.♕h4!, and Black is in real trouble: 14...♘c8 15.♗g5!

15...f6 (15...hxg5? loses to 16.♘xg5 ♖e8 17.♕h7+ ♔f8 18.♕xg6 ♕e7 19.♗g4!) 16.♗xh6, with an extra pawn in Stevic-Mohr, Austria 2011.

Another normal line is 6...e6 7.c3 ♘ge7 8.♗e3 0-0 and now 9.d4 gives both sides approximately equal chances.

7.c3

An excellent alternative is 7.♕e1 0-0 8.♕h4. A crude approach perhaps, but it is exactly in line with Black's play in the Ilyin-Zhenevsky Variation in the Dutch. 8...c4!? (trying to gain counterplay. 8...♗g4 9.♘bd2 ♖c8 10.c3 e6 11.h3 ♗xf3 12.♘xf3 ♘e8 13.♕xd8 ♖xd8 14.♗e3 f5?! 15.e5 dxe5 16.♗xc5 gave White a winning position in Ivkov-Rukavina, Bor 1976) 9.♔h1 cxd3 (9...♘b4 10.♘a3 cxd3 11.cxd3 ♘c6 12.f5! gxf5 13.♗h6 ♗xh6 14.♕xh6 ♘g4 15.♕g5+ ♔h8 16.exf5 ♘f6 17.♕f4, and White's position is easier to play. Stevic-C.Horvath, Sibenik 2010) 10.cxd3 ♗g4 11.♘c3 ♗xf3 12.♗xf3 ♕b6

Black appears as to have everything under control, but an excellent manoeuvre by McShane shows otherwise: 13.♗d1! (preparing both ♗b3 and ♖f3-h3!) 13...♕a6 14.♖f3 ♖fc8 15.♖h3 h5 16.f5 ♘e5 17.♗g5 Black has no counterplay on the queenside and is busted on the kingside. 17...♔f8 18.fxg6 fxg6 19.♗b3 ♘xd3 20.♖f3 1-0 McShane-Cheparinov, Novi Sad 2009. Black resigned, as he cannot prevent a devastating sacrifice on f6.

Let's return to 7.c3, but note that 7.♕e1 is an attractive alternative.

7...0-0 8.♔h1 b5

In my opinion, 8...c4! 9.♗e3 cxd3 10.♗xd3 is about equal.

9.a3 a5 10.♗e3 ♘g4 (10...a4)
11.♗g1 e5? 12.fxe5 ♘gxe5
13.♘xe5 ♘xe5 14.d4!

It is not clear what Yu Yangyi had missed. White wins the b5-pawn and Black does not gain sufficient compensation. Perhaps he had just underestimated White's bishops on e2 and g1? White won on move 42.

Igor Kovalenko
Sumiya Bilguun
Warsaw 2015 (1)

1.e4 c5 2.♗e2 e6

Playing a kind of Alekhine with 2...♘f6!? is interesting 3.e5 (3.d3 d5) 3...♘d5 4.♘f3!?.

3.f4 ♘c6 4.♘f3 d5 5.d3

Black now has the opportunity to play a queenless middlegame by taking on e4. However, removing the queens does not solve Black's problems, as we will see in Kovalenko-Olszewski.

5...g6

Black can also aim for a French setup: 5...♘f6 6.e5

and now:
– 6...♘g8 7.0-0 ♘h6 8.♗e3 ♘f5 9.♗f2 h5 10.c3 ♗d7 11.♘bd2 (11.a3!? a5 12.a4!) 11...♗e7 12.d4 c4 13.b4 b5 14.a4 a6 15.♕c2 was quite pleasant for White in Lagerman-Jovicic, Belgrade 2009.

– 6...♘d7 7.0-0 ♗e7 8.c4! ♘b6 9.♗e3 0-0 10.♘f2 f6 11.♘c3 fxe5 12.fxe5 ♖f5 13.♗g3 ♗d7 14.♘b5! ♗e8 15.a4 a6 16.♘d6 ♗xd6 17.exd6 ♘c8 18.♕d2 d4 (18...♘xd6 19.♕e3) 19.♗h4, and White had decent play for the pawn that he is going to lose; Vavulin-Smirnov, St Petersburg 2015. Note that the immediate 19...♕xd6 is met by 20.♘g5!, with a solid initiative.

6.0-0 ♗g7 7.♕e1 ♘ge7 8.c3

White has completed his 'preferred' scheme as noted in our introduction.

8...0-0 9.♘a3 a6

9...d4 10.♘c2 dxc3 11.bxc3 b6 12.♖b1 ♗a6 13.c4 ♕d7 14.♕h4 is slightly more comfortable for White; Rotstein-Spirin, Metz 2011.

10.♘c2 d4?!

10...b5 11.e5 (11.♕f2!? looks good) 11...f6 12.exf6 ♗xf6 13.♘e3 e5? (13...♗g7 14.♘g4 ♕d6 15.♗d2 is about even) 14.fxe5 ♘xe5 15.♘xe5 ♗xe5 Jasim-Adnan, Abu Dhabi 2000, and now White could have gained an edge with 16.♖xf8+ ♔xf8 17.♗f3 ♗b7 18.♘g4! (18.♘xd5 ♗xh2+) 18...♗g7 19.♗h6!.

11.♗d2 b5

Or 11...dxc3 12.♗xc3, with a plus.

12.cxd4 cxd4

Black cannot keep control of the d4-square with 12...♘xd4 13.♘cxd4 ♗xd4+ 14.♘xd4 ♕xd4+ 15.♕f2! ♕xb2 (15...♕xf2+ 16.♔xf2, and c5 has become weak) 16.♗e3.

13.♖c1 ♗b7

White has won the opening battle. He has a marked positional advantage. The remainder of the game looks like a series of positional exercises.

White to play.

14.♘a1!

The knight is heading for c5, where it will be a real beast!

14...a5 15.♘b3 ♕b6 16.♘c5 ♖fd8 17.♕h4 ♗c8 18.♗d1!? **a4?! 19.b4 f6** 19...axb3 20.♗xb3 was the point of 18.♗d1. Suddenly the bishop enters the fray.

20.a3 ♖f8

White to play.

21.♗c2! Beautiful! The bishop is heading for the diagonal a2-g8.

21...♕d8 22.♗b1 ♕d6 23.♗a2 ♖a7 Material is still equal and yet White is completely winning: 24.e5, 24.f5 and 24.♕h3 are all very strong, but Kovalenko's play in the game was more than sufficient too.

**Igor Kovalenko
Michal Olszewski**
Warsaw 2015 (3)

In this game we will see that playing for a queen-less middle game leaves White with the better chances.

1.e4 c5 2.♗e2 g6

2...♘c6 3.f4 d5 4.d3 dxe4 5.dxe4 ♕xd1+ 6.♗xd1 ♘f6 7.♘c3 ♗g4!? 8.♗e3

8...e6 9.h3 ♗xd1 10.♖xd1 ♘b4?! 11.♖d2 ♖d8 12.♘f3 ♗e7 13.g4 White has a space advantage and better pieces, Khusnutdinov-Yuan, Al Ain 2015. 2...e6 3.f4 ♘c6 4.♘f3 d5 5.d3 dxe4 (5...♘f6) 6.dxe4 ♕xd1+ 7.♗xd1

At the first glance, you might think that Black has equalized after trading the queens, but White has more space, e4 and f4 control a lot of important squares, and the pawn on c5 isn't all that great. A few examples simply to get a feel for the position.

– 7...b6 8.c3 ♗b7 9.♗e3 0-0-0 10.♘bd2 ♘f6 11.♗c2 ♗e7 12.h3 ♘d7 13.0-0-0, and due to his space advantage the queenless middlegame is better for White, Ernst-L.van Foreest, Vlissingen 2015.

– 7...♘f6 8.e5! ♘d5 9.c4 ♘db4 10.♔e2 ♗e7 11.♘c3 0-0 12.a3 ♘a6 13.♘b5 left White clearly better in Stevic-Sanikidze, Plovdiv 2010.

3.f4 ♗g7 4.♘f3 d5

While it is also possible, of course, to play 5.e5 or 5.exd5 here, the modest-looking **5.d3** is actually quite strong. White keeps his pawn centre in place. And trading queens once again doesn't solve all Black's problems.

5...dxe4 6.dxe4 ♕xd1+ 7.♗xd1

b6 (7...♘c6) **8.♘a3 ♗a6 9.c3 ♘d7** (9...♘c6) **10.♗e2** Kovalenko keeps it simple; it is useful to gain control of the light squares on the queenside.

10...♗xe2 11.♔xe2 0-0-0 **12.♗e3 ♘h6 13.h3!**

White can quietly improve his position, while Black is lacking counterplay.

13...f6 Playing the knight to f7 and possibly to d6 is actually Black's best option, so there is no need to condemn the 'ugly' 13...f6.

14.♘c4 ♘f7 15.g4 ♘d6 16.♘cd2 16.♘xd6+ exd6 17.♘d2 is also better for White, but why give Black more breathing space?

16...♔c7 17.♖ag1 ♔c6 18.h4 **♖he8** (18...e5 19.f5) **19.c4!?** (19.h5) **19...e5 20.f5 ♔c7** 20...♖h8 21.fxg6 hxg6 22.h5 gxh5 was more tenacious; 20...gxf5 21.gxf5 is unattractive.

21.a3 (21.fxg6! hxg6 22.h5±) **21...♗f8** (21...♖h8) **22.fxg6 hxg6** **23.h5 g5**

White now has a strategically winning position: a protected passed pawn, and a superior bishop, not to mention the gaping holes on d5 and f5. He won on move 56. ∎

A coach's view

Mikhail Antipov U-20 World Junior Champion

In a dramatic last round Russia's Mikhail Antipov caught up with Jan Krzysztof Duda and edged out the Polish favourite to take the title on tiebreak. **Loek van Wely** travelled to the World Junior Championship in Khanty-Mansiysk as the coach of the Dutch delegation. With wide experience in the trade our reporter freely shares his coaching insights.

This story goes way back, as far back as 2004 when the World Junior Championship was held in Kochi, India. The name of the coach: Loek van Wely. The name of the victims he accompanied: Jan Smeets and Erwin l'Ami. To be honest, I have hardly any recollection of what kind of experience it was. But the same Erwin l'Ami was approached by the Dutch Chess Federation to go to this year's World Junior Championship in Siberia as the coach of our hopefuls Benjamin Bok and Jorden van Foreest. Perhaps Erwin wanted to go, but he found it impossible to say no to his lovely wife Alina, who had booked a cultural trip to Mexico at the same time. Erwin, possibly still traumatized from the trip to India in 2004, didn't hesitate for a

moment and immediately recommended me as his substitute.

In fact that suited me very well, as after all I had planned a trip to El

> 'Not only did I draw against a fish, I also believe that young guns should take any chance to play hard against top GMs, just to test themselves.'

Salvador to visit my in-laws ☺. I said to my wife: 'Listen honey, I am so sorry, but I have to work. Those guys really need me, what can I do? This is a clear case of force majeure! My only problem was that I don't know how to look innocent. Well, maybe I should have taken that big smile off my face, that would have been a good start!

Although I am not an expert in the coaching field, I still have had a lot of coaching experience, on either side. For instance, I know that to get along well with your pupil can be a big plus. With Benjamin Bok (aka Bokito, but due to the connotations this nickname has in Dutch, you better call him Benji) I had quite some history. The first time we played was at the Dutch Championship in 2010.

SI 41.14 – B43
Benjamin Bok
Loek van Wely
Eindhoven 2010

Benji had entered the tournament on a wildcard. As you will see he was using his wildcard to its full extent!
1.e4 c5 2.♘f3 e6 3.d4 cxd4 4.♘xd4 a6 5.♘c3 ♕c7 6.♗d3 ♘f6 7.0-0 ♗c5 8.♘b3 ♗e7 9.f4 d6

10.e5 This came as an unpleasant surprise. Carlsen played 10.a4 against me in 1996, and we got a type of position I liked. Nevertheless I lost.
10...dxe5 11.fxe5

11...♕xe5
11...♘fd7 was the alternative but after 12.♕g4 g6 13.♗h6 ♘xe5 14.♕g3 ♘bc6 15.♗e4 Black is facing serious problems.
12.♗f4 ♕h5 13.♗e2

13...♕g6
Black's options are limited.
13...♕h4 14.g3 ♕h3 15.♘e4 e5 (15...♘xe4 16.♗g4 ♕xf1+ 17.♕xf1 and White is just much better) 16.♘d6+ looks too dangerous.

14.♗d3

14.h4! h6 15.h5 ♕h7 16.♗d6 ♘c6 17.♗xe7 ♔xe7 18.♗f3 was the real test, and to make things worse, Benji knew that!

14...♕h5 15.♗e2 ♕g6

16.♗d3? Only this is the real blunder, since now Black can claim a draw! Not only that, during the following sequence Benji also offered me a draw twice. But that day I had no intentions to go easy on him. Also worth noting is that that day my heartbeat was being monitored. Once I had realized that Benji was going for a draw, my heartbeat took a serious hit.

16...♕h5 17.♗e2 ♕g6 18.♗d3? ♕h5 19.♗e2 ♕g6 20.♗d3? ♕h5 21.♗e2 ♕g6 22.♗d3? ♕h5 23.♗e2 ♕g6 24.♗d3? ♕h5 25.♗e2 ♕g6 26.♗d3? ♕h5 27.♗e2 ♕g6 28.♗d3? ♕h5 29.♗e2 ♕g6 30.♗d3? ♕h5 31.♗e2 ♕g6 32.♗d3? ♕h5 33.♗e2 ♕g6 34.♗d3? ♕h5 35.♗e2 ♕g6 36.♗d3? ♕h5 37.♗e2 ♕g6

Finally Benji got the message and claimed a draw. My request for a reconstruction was waived away. Of course, I was livid. Not only did

I draw against a fish, which shattered my chances to win the Dutch championship, I also believe that young guns should take any chance to play hard against top GMs, just to test themselves. Also, I have never seen anybody making so many bad moves, I count at least more than 10, and still making a draw comfortably against a 2600+ GM!

Needless to say, since then Benji had the red flag on him, and although we didn't play for many years, he was one of my favourite guys to tease. We also had some training sessions before he fell into the hands of the wrong trainer. And on top of that he was supporting the wrong football club! Luckily for him the tide changed when we met again in 2014 Dutch Championship and he realized that he could beat me.

With Jorden I have also had a training session. I realized that he has quite some potential (but also many weaknesses, which is both a good and a bad sign). He comes from a chess family, which is fine (unless you have a little brother whose name is Lucas).

Let me say a few words of my work as a coach or second. In 1996 I was invited to work with the Kamskys, Gata and his father Rustam; for Gata's FIDE World Championship match in Elista. An opportunity to work on the highest level, although it was not so simple. First of all, father Kamsky was always deciding which opening was going to be played. Secondly, he claimed the house where we were staying was bugged, so we couldn't say the moves! Last but not least, sometimes Rustam was intervening in our analysis. To which I would have to say things like: 'Sorry Rustam, your idea is very good, but unfortunately your move is illegal...'

> **'I am still curious how the guy managed to remember all the rubbish I analysed for him, but that was his problem.'**

In 2002 I worked with Veselin Topalov. Also highly interesting, I especially liked the working method. Veselin and I analysing over the board, and Silvio (Danailov) with the computer shouting some moves. The work may not have been 100% correct, but was full of ideas.

In 2007 it was Vladimir Kramnik that I worked with. His motto was basically: Analyze everything till the end! Unfortunately, I didn't have the authority to tell him: 'Listen up, dude, that's not how it works!' Still, it worked pretty well for him. I am still curious how the guy managed to remember all the rubbish I analysed for him, but that was his problem ☺.

But the work I had to do was killing, making you want to quit working on chess, or chess in general. I started

With the positions he got, Benjamin Bok should 'at least have taken silver'.

to think, if this is what my life is going to be like, my life won't be too funny!

But what I did enjoy during our joint analysis was driving him nuts by switching on my engines the whole time (Junior and Rybka in those days) while poor Vlad was relying on his Fritzy-boy and got slaughtered the whole time.

It seems that the player-coach relationship is a lot about belief. Not only has the coach to believe in his pupil, the pupil also has to believe what the coach is saying. Or pretend to... During the Kamsky-Karpov match, I once witnessed how a furious father Kamsky (after Gata had lost with White in a Russian Game) slammed the black rooks from h8 and a8 on e2 and d2. You will understand that something had gone wrong in that game. Karpov, who was unable to castle after having played Kf8, still managed to activate his rooks somehow. I had to bite my tongue not to burst out laughing, because this was so ridiculous. I don't know what was going through Gata's mind then, I guess he was just waiting for the storm to calm.

I have also witnessed Silvio addressing Veselin, after he had lost a game in the Amber tournament, and suggesting some really bad moves that he should have played. And Veselin just nodded and agreed!

Once I got indirect proof that a pupil wasn't listening. The pupil, a native American (Caruana), apparently had told his trainer that his English was very good. The whole night I was thinking: how could he say that? The trainer's English is not good at all! Then it dawned on me: he is not listening at all and that's why he has 2800!

Anyway, what was my task in Khanty-Mansiysk then?

1. Being a cheerleader? According to Paul Truong there were serious coaches and cheerleaders during the World Cup in Baku, a sneer at the Wesley So camp. I believe that a good cheerleader is quite important as well. After all it's a mind game, so you need to feel well. Interestingly, he also gave a peek in what a normal day of a 'serious' coach looks like. All in all, it contained like 12 hours of preparation! I don't know how Susan Polgar manages to do that, but me, after 6 hours of intense work, I start to faint. To cut a long story short, in Baku it was 'cheerleader' vs. 'serious coach' 1-0.

2. Playing the scarecrow? Trying to scare the opponents and take them out of their comfort zone? Making them less confident, and making them not to play their usual openings? Of course, this coach prefers to sleep during the night, rather than work on some lines which probably won't happen anyway.

3. Selling old analysis as new? Probably what I sold back then in 2004 to Smeets and l'Ami, maybe I should try to sell it again? I remember when I saw Giri playing one of my ideas in Wijk aan Zee in 2010, an idea I had analysed when I was working with Vladimir Chuchelov, who was then working with Anish. I asked Anish: 'Did you get my file?' To which he replied: 'No, the coach showed me this new idea this morning...'

I believe that first of all these kids need a good mental coach. Benji needs a confidence boost, while Jorden may sometimes require some bashing, just to keep him in line. Of course some preparation is required, but by choosing the right opening most of the work has already been done.

So how did it go in reality? In reality the coach, during the games, was banging his head against the wall nonstop and in the end I was just mentally exhausted. They both ended in a massive tie for fourth place. Benji had so many good positions, he should have taken at least silver. Jorden was too erratic to have claims for more, but once he becomes more consistent he will be very dangerous.

MARIA EMELIANOVA

'Once Jorden van Foreest becomes more consistent, he will be very dangerous.'

Someone who looked very consistent to me was Jan Krzysztof Duda. For me, he was the clear favourite. He won a very interesting game against Grigoryan.

KP 11.9 – C48
Jan-Krzysztof Duda
Karen Grigoryan
Khanty-Mansiysk 2015 (6)

1.e4 e5 2.♘f3 ♘c6 3.♘c3 ♘f6 4.♗b5 ♘d4 5.♗a4 ♗c5 6.♘xe5 0-0 7.♘d3 ♗b6 8.e5 ♘e8

9.0-0 More common is 9.♘d5. **9...d5** Or 9...c6. **10.♔h1** 10.b3!? looks interesting, but of course I wouldn't dare to make such a suggestion without checking it with my computer at the risk of being laughed at.
10...c6 Black already looks very comfortable here.

11.♘e2 ♛h4 12.♘g3

12...♗g4?! I don't like this move. In view of White's lag in development, Black needs to open up the position with 12...f6.

13.f3 ♗e6 14.c3 ♘f5 15.♘e2 d4 16.♗c2 ♖d8 Of course, White still has to be very careful.

17.c4?! And White blinks first. Don't ask me why 17.a4 a5 18.♛e1 is better than 17.♛e1, but the silicon monster thinks so.

17.g4 ♘e7 18.♘ef4 is another suggestion, but I would be very hesitant to play this.

17...f6?!

18.b3 18.g4 would have been more aggressive: 18...♘e7 19.b3

Top-seed and clear favourite Jan-Krzysztof Duda was leading throughout the championship, but saw the title go up in smoke on the final day.

fxe5 20.♗a3 e4! (forced, as otherwise White consolidates with ♘g3) 21.♘df4 ♗c8 22.♗xe4, and White is better.

18...fxe5 19.♗a3 ♖f6 20.♛e1 ♛h6

21.♘xe5

Once again Jan-Krzysztof refrains from playing g4. I understand it's complicated and you will have to calculate hard, but he should be able to do so. Apart from that, young boys are normally not afraid (and not so wise either). After 21.g4 ♗c7 22.f4 e4 23.g5 exd3 24.gxh6 dxc2 White may be better, but the position may not be to everyone's taste.

21...d3 22.♘g4

22...dxe2! The right moment to sac the queen! After 22...♛g5 23.♘c3 ♖g6 (also 23...dxc2 24.♘e4 ♛h5 25.♘exf6+ ♖xf6 26.♛xe6+ ♔h8 27.♛e5 leaves White on top) 24.♘e4 ♛h5 25.♗d1 White should be solid.

23.♘xh6+ ♖xh6 24.♖f2?!

Better was 24.♖g1.

24...♗xf2 25.♛xf2 ♖xd2 26.♛c5

26...♘ed6 Here 26...♖f6 was stronger, and for a concrete reason (it's not only defending against the mate).

27.♛a5?!

Better was 27.♖e1 ♖xc2 28.g4 (once again, this move). However, things are far from over: 28...♖c3! 29.gxf5 ♗xf5, and Black's strong initiative should guarantee him at least a draw.

27...♖xc2 28.♛d8+ ♔f7 29.♛c7+ ♔e8 30.♖e1 ♖d2 31.♔g1

31...♖d1?

From here on in, Karen is starting to drift. Much more sense made 31...♗d7, with the idea of coordinating his pieces by playing ...♖e6, when Black's rook on d2 is free to hover around.

32.♔f2 ♖xe1 33.♔xe1

The exchange of the e1 rook for the d2 one clearly favours White.

33...♘c8 34.♔xe2 ♗d7 35.♕xb7 ♖xh2 36.♔f2 ♖h6 37.♗c5

Now Black's pieces lack any coordination and there are no targets in White's camp to attack.

37...♘fd6 38.♕b8 a6 39.♕a8 ♖f6 40.♔g1 a5 41.♗d4 ♖g6 42.♕xa5 ♘f5 43.♗f2 ♖d6 44.♕e1+ ♔f7 45.♗c5 ♖e6 46.♕d2 ♔e8 47.a4 ♘fd6 48.♗a3

And here Grigoryan realized that he will be unable to stop the a-pawn in the long run. Black resigned.

But there was still one guy left that he had to shake off: Mikhail Antipov! In fact I don't know much about him, apart from the fact that I always see him in the Spanish team competition

and that he is always winning against our team. Still, it was easier to imagine that one of my boys would take the title rather than he, but then this happened.

IG 2.15 – C54
**Mikhail Antipov
Jorden van Foreest**
Khanty-Mansiysk 2015 (8)

The downfall of Jorden was the making of Mikhail.
1.e4 e5 2.♘f3 ♘c6 3.♗c4 ♘f6 4.d3 ♗c5 5.0-0 0-0 6.c3 d5 7.exd5 ♘xd5 8.b4

I don't really believe this can be any good, but at least it leads to some non-standard positions. And I guess he wanted to take us out of book.

8...♗e7 9.b5 ♘a5 10.♗xd5 ♕xd5 11.c4 ♕d7

We hadn't particularly prepared for this line, but Jorden played fast and confidently nonetheless. I just wish he had taken his time later on....
12.♘c3 f6 13.♘d5 ♗d8 14.♗a3 ♖e8 15.♖c1 Thus far, I was very happy: an unbalanced position, which should suit Jorden well.

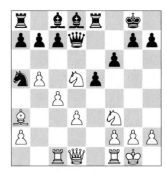

15...a6 16.b6

A necessity, otherwise White's pawn structure will be blown up.

16...cxb6 16...c6 also wins a pawn, but leaves the knight on a5 in a very awkward spot. Understandably, Jorden wants to avoid that. On the other hand, it leaves the white knight on d5 in the saddle for a while: 17.♘c3 ♗xb6 18.c5.

17.♘d2 f5 18.f4

This is one of those very crucial moments when Jorden really should have taken his time. The return would have been huge.

18...e4?!

Playing with fire. I like 18...b5, simply trying to destroy White's structure: 19.fxe5 bxc4 20.dxc4 b5, with ...♗b7

next, and Black should be happy.
18...exf4 is another good option, just keeping things under control.

19.♖e1 I wonder what Jorden had in mind after 19.dxe4, because 19...fxe4 20.♖e1, with another knight heading to the centre of the board, doesn't really excite me.

19...b5 20.dxe4

20...fxe4??
Once again a capital sin, allowing the knight to come to e4. Of course now it's getting concrete, but with Black's queenside locked up, I would have double-checked, or even triple-checked. But going by Jorden's speed of play, I doubt he did.
20...♕f7 would have been more thematic. Now it will be thematic, too!

21.♘xe4 ♘xc4 22.♕h5 ♖e6
Black just needs one more move to consolidate...

23.f5!!
The only move, but you need only one move to win.

23...♕xd5 Maybe Jorden thought 23.f5 wouldn't work because of the text-move, but the next move is the real killer.

24.♘g5!!

24...♗xg5 There is nothing else.
25.♕e8+ ♖xe8 26.♖xe8+ ♔f7 27.♖f8 Mate.

The big showdown came in the last round. Duda was still leading by half a point. Unfortunately, he was playing back against Bok. Not only that, but a bad opening choice resulted in a passive and bad position. Thanks to Benji he managed to draw.

So Antipov needed to win to tie for first. Which he did and then he took the title on tiebreak, by the smallest of margins, I guess that a game between (no offense) players from Zambia and Congo decided the issue.

CK 4.2 – B12
**Mikhail Antipov
Francesco Rambaldi**
Khanty-Mansiysk 2015 (13)

1.e4 c6 2.d4 d5 3.e5 ♗f5 4.♘d2 e6 5.♘b3 ♘d7 6.♘f3 h6 7.♗e2 ♘e7 8.0-0 g5

This is a topical line these days. When Benjamin Bok faced Francesco, he decided to side-step this line.
9.♘e1 ♕c7 10.♘d3 ♘g6 11.♗d2 0-0-0

This move makes little sense, unless you like to provoke some action in the centre.
12.a4 f6 13.exf6 ♗d6 14.g3 ♖df8 15.♘dc5 ♗xc5 16.♘xc5 ♘xc5 17.dxc5 ♗h3 18.♖e1 ♖xf6 19.♗g4 ♗xg4 20.♕xg4

20...h5! Not afraid to sac a pawn. Besides opening the g-file, Black also mobilizes his centre.

21.♕xg5 ♕f7 22.♕e3 e5 23.b4

Not sure what he is doing. White's attack is definitely going nowhere.

23...♖f8 24.♖f1 h4 25.♕e2 e4 26.♗c3 f3 27.♗d4 ♕d7 28.♔h1 ♕g4 29.♖fe1 e3! 30.♗xe3 hxg3 31.hxg3

So far Francesco has played an excellent game. It's really amazing that White somehow survives this!

And there he goes! Mikhail Antipov, the 18-year-old GM from Moscow, is the new World Junior Champion after a dramatic last round.

31...♘h4 The simplest way to win seemed to be 31...♕h3+ 32.♔g1 ♘e5 33.♕f1 ♖xg3+. I can't argue with the text-move; after all, the engine gives +11 for Black. Still, Black has to make some not so evident moves.

32.♔h2

32...d4??

Instead, 32...♖e8, followed by ...♘f5, is crushing. However, who wants to move the rook from f8, where it's placed well. And to move the knight away from h4, where you've just put it?

33.♗f4

33...♖xf2+??

Black now had to be content with a (much) better endgame. But in time-trouble it is hard to change gears: 33...♘g6 34.♕e6+ ♕xe6 35.♖xe6 ♖xf2+ 36.♔g1 ♘xf4 37.gxf4 ♖2xf4 38.♖e2 a5!.

34.♕xf2 ♘f3+ 35.♔g2 ♖xf4 36.♖e8+ ♔d7 37.♖ae1

With a nasty counter-threat.

37...♘xe1+? Now the roles have been reversed. It's Black who should settle for a (much) worse rook ending with 37...♖f7 38.♖1e4 ♘h4+ 39.♔h1! ♕xe4+ 40.♖xe4 ♖xf2 41.♖xd4+ ♔e6 42.gxh4. **38.♕xe1 ♖f7 39.♖b8 ♕f3+ 40.♔g1 ♖f8 41.♖xb7+ ♔c8 42.♖xa7 ♔b8 43.♖e7 ♖d8 44.b5 d3 45.♕e5+ ♔a8 46.♖a7+ ♔xa7 47.♕c7+ ♔a8 48.♕xd8+ ♔b7 49.♕d7+ ♔b8 50.♕xd3**

Black resigned. What drama! ∎

Ladies First

Why put your queen on d2 when your bishop is still on c1? **ARTHUR VAN DE OUDEWEETERING** explores an unusual battery that can be highly effective.

Wasn't it 'minor pieces first'? Then why should you move your queen right in the way of an undeveloped bishop on c1? Let's find out where it could be heading for.

David Navara
Jan Timman
Wijk aan Zee 2015

1.d4 ♘f6 2.c4 e6 3.♘f3 ♗b4+ 4.♘bd2 0-0 5.a3 ♗e7 6.e4 d5 7.e5 ♘fd7 8.♗d3 c5 9.h4 g6 10.h5 cxd4 11.♘b3 dxc4 12.♗xc4 b5 13.♗d3 ♗b7

14.♕d2!? Not complying with the basic rules of development, but putting up a reversed battery with the queen as the most forward piece. Strange? Wait and see, soon you will get used to this blocking of the bishop's diagonal. The automatic move was 14.♗h6, devel-oping with tempo. Yet Navara, having opted for a straightforward opening set-up, consistently continues with the caveman approach. Concrete calcula-tions do the talking here. **14...♘xe5?** And with immediate success! The point is that after 14...♗xf3 15.♕h6!, White's attacking potential turns out to be suf-ficient for a deadly assault. 14...♖e8 runs into 15.hxg6 fxg6 16.♕h6 ♘f8 17.♗xg6!. The radical 14...g5 seems to be the only viable alternative, although White's position remains better, for example after 15.♗c2, preparing the more traditional battery with ♕d3. **15.♘xe5 ♕d5 16.♘f3 g5 17.♘xg5 f5 18.♖h3 ♕xg2 19.♗f1** 1-0.

14.♕d2 may have surprised Timman, but there was a similar example in the same line: 11.cxd5 ♘c5 12.♗b1 exd5 13.b4 ♘e6 14.♘b3 ♘c6 15.♕d2!, and Black was equally helpless in Mirosh-nichenko-Andreev, Al Ain 2013.

You might reason that today's calculat-ing engines inspire us to find and play such concrete moves. And that for-merly we could easily pass by this kind of moves just because they do not seem 'natural' enough. This might well be true in general, but the following exam-ple dates from the 1970s, and here the queen found its way to the kingside in exactly the same manner.

Velimirovic-Rukavina
Novi Sad 1975

Here you would probably be itching to play the natural ♗h6 right away. Dragoljub Velimirovic thought oth-erwise:

14.♕d2!? The queen hastens to par-ticipate in the attack. Not as direct an approach as in the Navara game, where the h1-rook was also threaten-ing to take part, but still pretty straight-forward. **14...♖fe8 15.♕h6 ♗f8 16.♕h4** In three moves White has transferred his queen to the kingside. Black now tries to prove that the queen has been exposed too early, but this utterly fails. **16...♘ce7? 17.♘eg5 h6 18.♘h3?!** Remarkable! Instead White could have struck with 18.♘xf7! ♔xf7 19.♘e5+ ♔g8 20.♗xh6, and White is ready to collect a third pawn on g6, with an ongoing attack. Yet in the game White also obtained a winning posi-tion quickly after **18...♔h7?! 19.♘e5 ♘f5 20.♗xf5 exf5 21.♘g5+ ♔g8 22.♘gxf7** (1-0, 35)

Talking about the 1970s, there is this famous example of Black's weak dark squares on the kingside inducing the white queen to explode into action. It's from the final stages of the match which later turned out to be a battle for the World Championship title due to Fischer's withdrawal. With four games to go, Karpov had a comfortable two-point lead.

Kortchnoi-Karpov
Moscow (21st match game) 1974
position after 10...g6

It seems that Petrosian had advised Karpov not to play this particular line anymore. **11.♕d2!** An exclamation mark from Kortchnoi, who selected this game for his *Best Games with White* volume. He added: 'A move the true value of which was recognised by many venerable commentators, including former World Champion Botvinnik, who even expressed the suggestion that I had prepared it at home. But I could not have anticipated all of Karpov's dubious moves!' Indeed, Karpov's light-hearted reply allowed a quick finish: **11...♘xd5 12.♗xd5 ♖b8?** A young Kasparov happened to be present and witnessed the following blow from nearby, as vividly narrated in *My Great Predecessors* Part V. Neither he nor Kortchnoi supplies an alternative for Black, although the elimination of one attacking piece with 12...♘a5 should have kept Black in the race.

13.♘xh7! ♖e8 13...♔xh7 14.♕h6+ ♔g8 15.♕xg6+ ♔h8 16.♕h6+ ♔g8 17.♗e4. **14.♕h6 ♘e5 15.♘g5 ♗xg5 16.♗xg5 ♕xg5 17.♕xg5 ♗xd5 18.0-0 ♗xc4 19.f4** 1-0.

Obviously, ...g7-g6 without a fianchettoed bishop may be a clear incentive for the reversed battery. Occasionally, ...h7-h6 may do the same, as witness the following fragment from four years earlier, this time with Kortchnoi in the role of defender.

Tukmakov-Kortchnoi
Riga 1970
position after 18...♔f8

19.♕d2!? The attentive reader will notice that this diagram would have fitted perfectly in my column in New In Chess 2015/5: 19.♗xh6! gxh6 20.♕d2. Tukmakov feared there would be no follow-up after 20...♕b4 21.♕xh6+ ♔e7 22.♖f3 ♘bd5 23.♘xd5+ ♘xd5 24.♖xf7+ ♔d6, but after 25.♗f5 things look pretty desperate for Black. Still, his actual choice provides too much fun to leave this example out. **19...♘bd5 20.♗g6!?** This yielded the desired spectacular effect after Black's reply. Meanwhile, the other tactical motif would have been the better choice: 20.♖xg7 ♔xg7 21.♕xh6+ ♔g8, and now for instance 22.♘xd5 ♖xc1+ 23.♕xc1 ♘xd5 24.♖a3, when after 24...♕b4 25.♖f3! ♕e1+ 26.♕xe1 ♖xe1 27.♖xf7 the mating attack continues! Of course, this rook sacrifice would have demanded quite some over-the-board calculation. **20...♗e8?** 20...♗c7 was called for, intending to eliminate White's important centralized knight.

21.♕xh6! A wonderful move to play! **21...♕b4** 21...gxh6 22.♗xh6+ ♔g8 23.♗e4+ ♔h8 24.♗g7+ ♔g8 25.♗xf6+ ♔f8 26.♘xd5 exd5 27.♗xe7+ ♔xe7 28.♗f5 leaves White two pawns up. **22.♕h8+ ♘e7 23.♕xg7 ♕xd4 24.♘d3 ♗xc3 25.bxc3 ♘xc3 26.♗a3+ ♔d7 27.♖e1** and White won.

This last example may be exceptional; much more common is the following manoeuvre, which even leaves Black's kingside pawn structure uncompromised.

Ni Hua-Bu Xiangzhi
Xinghua Jiangsu 2011
position after 10...♕d7

11.♕d2!? White has more options; the natural looking 11.♗f4 being one of them. **11...0-0 12.♕f4 f6 13.♕g3** This is the idea. Here the queen is much more active than on d1, of course. **13...♗f7 14.♗f4! fxe5 15.♗xe5!** and White's annoying pressure has already yielded a pawn. **15...♗g4 16.♗xc7 ♖bf8 17.♘e5 ♘xe5 18.♗xe5 ♗c5 19.♗d4 ♗xd4 20.cxd4 ♖xf2 21.♕h4 h6 22.♖e7** and White won.

So do look out for this unconventional(?) possibility to activate your strongest piece – sometimes the bishop can wait! ∎

Understand first, calculate later

'It's been raining books on me this past month!', **MATTHEW SADLER** tells us. And our reviewer's enthusiasm is not limited to the number of books that reached him.

Lots to get through this time! We start with Russell Enterprise's reprint of the classic work *The Art of Sacrifice* by Rudolf Spielmann. To my shame, it's a book I've never actually got around to reading before so I was very happy when this one landed on my doorstep! It's also a classic Mark Dvoretsky recommends in one of his articles in his new book *For Friends and Colleagues Volume II*. Spielmann was one of the strongest players in the first half of the 20th century. Just like Tartakower, he was a little too lightweight to challenge the might of the greats like Capablanca and Alekhine, but he was an interesting and creative player who – particularly in his youth – was famed for his bold attacking play. *The Art of Sacrifice* is an attempt to classify and categorise the sacrifice in chess, using Spielmann's own games as examples.

I've read it through a couple of times now and I love it. Spielmann's approach is sober and realistic – he acknowledges that a number of sacrifices may not be sound while stressing the practical difficulties that the defender faces – and rings true to these relatively modern ears. That's

not a bad achievement for a book written 80 years ago! Many of his insights have stuck in my mind – I'll give a couple here.

The first and most important classification according to Spielmann is the difference between 'sham' sacrifices

> 'In such heated situations, I make an effort to take a step back and understand in words – rather than in variations – what I'm planning.'

and 'real' sacrifices. Sham sacrifices 'involve losses of material only for a definable amount of time. In the case of real sacrifices, the amount of time required for recovering the material is not clear. There a sham (temporary) sacrifice involves no risk. After

a series of forced moves, the player either recovers the invested material with advantage or else even mates his opponent. The consequences of the sacrifice were foreseen from the first. Properly speaking, there is no sacrifice, only an advantageous business deal.'

I like collecting such clear, succinct explanations for use during games. One of the biggest challenges during practical play is to keep track of your risk exposure. In the heat of the moment – especially in tense, tight situations when you are desperate to make the most of your position – it's easy to start calculating sequences of committal decisions without quite appreciating what you would be taking on. In such situations, I make an effort to take a step back and understand in words – rather than in variations – what I'm planning. For example, am I making a sham sacrifice or a real sacrifice? If the latter then I need to understand that I'm raising the stakes, and that I'll need to raise my energy level to cope with that. Am I ready for such a fight? The more ready-made descriptions you have at your fingertips, the easier it is to describe your efforts in words and thus understand what you are doing!

Another explanation that struck a chord was Spielmann's image for how the value of pieces changes continually according to the position in front of you: 'All chess units have, in the language of the stock exchange, two prices, the par value and the quoted rate. The par value represents the absolute (1 point for a pawn, 3 points for a knight or bishop), the price from day to day of the relative values. The absolute value forms the basis on which exchanges are made; the relative value is the decisive factor for positional play, for combinations and especially for sacrifices. The simpler the position, the more the absolute value carries weight. The more complicated the position, the more does the relative value gain in importance. In the original position, the absolute value practically counts alone, the relative value only arises in the course of the game. The lead is given by the absolute value for it is enduring as against the relative value which is variable and transient.' This is the most evocative explanation I have read of how sacrifices or unusual positional decisions seek to exploit or create a temporary disruption in the value of pieces. It also underlines the risk that such a decision entails: if the sacrifice achieves nothing, then the absolute values of the pieces will reassert themselves.

Funnily enough, the first things I thought about when I read this were a couple of examples quoted in Mark Dvoretsky's book *For Friends and Colleagues Volume II*. First of all, this position from the stunning game Anand-Carlsen, Linares 2007.

Anand-Carlsen
Morelia/Linares 2007
position after 22...♘a8

Anand considered 23.♘e1 here (with the idea of ♘d3-c5, sacrificing the knight for 2 enormous passed pawns) but felt that 23...♗g5 would give Black some relief after 24.♕d2 ♗xe3

The Art of Sacrifice in Chess
by Rudolf Spielmann
Russell Enterprises 2015
★★★★☆

25.♕xe3 ♕b8. He therefore decided on a preliminary move to stop Black from exchanging the dark-squared bishops with ...♗g5
23.♕d2 ♕b8 24.♗g5

What?? Dvoretsky quotes Anand's annotations 'This seems illogical. You first avoid the bishop exchange and then you force it yourself. There is no grand reason I can give, it is purely a tactical thing. It seems less effective to exchange the bishops with the knight on e1. But here Black wants to play ...♖c8 and once Black manages to swap off the rooks or to defend himself against direct threats, the advantage is gone and you can offer a draw. So it is very important to act quickly. 24.♗g5 relies on two things. One is that 24...f6 is impossible because of 25.♘xe5 and wins. The second is that after swapping, there are some very direct lines, as you will see, involving ♕h6.'

After having read Spielmann, you would say that with the knight on e1, Black's dark-squared bishop was worth less to White than his own dark-squared bishop, so White avoided the exchange. With the White knight on f3, White queen on

d2 and Black queen on b8, Black's dark-squared bishop was suddenly worth more to White than his own bishop – the relative value of the bishops had changed in this specific position – and so White offered the exchange of bishops after acting to prevent it on the previous move. Great positional awareness from Vishy. Enjoy the rest of this stunning game as well – Vishy's been around for so long, you forget sometimes how good he is!
24...♗xg5 25.♘xg5 ♖c8 26.♖f1 h6 27.♘e6 ♔h7 28.f4 ♕a7+ 29.♔h2 ♗e8 30.f5 gxf5 31.exf5 f6 32.♖e1 ♘c7 33.♖c1 ♗d7 34.♖c3 e4 35.♖g3 ♘xe6 36.dxe6 ♗e8 37.e7 ♗h5 38.♕xd6 1-0

The second game is also a game of Anand's.

Ivanchuk-Anand
Linares 1992 (1st match game)
position after 22...♖h3

Again Dvoretsky quotes Anand's remarks: 'Black appears to have committed a whole list of positional sins: allowing doubled f-pawns, giving White an outside passed h-pawn and exchanging his good bishop with ...♗c4. Yet, he is better. Paradoxical? Yes, but this does not mean that the old positional rules have been suspended for the course of this game. Black's play depends on two things: First of all, his long-term aim is to exchange his d-pawn for White's e-pawn by ...d5 and to exchange his f6-pawn for White's g-pawn either by ...f5 or by forcing White to play g5. Then, he will be left with two con-

nected central pawns, supported by his king, whereas White will have pawns on h2 and c2 that are not going anywhere. Secondly he can only put his plan into action because he has the initiative, and especially as the rook on h3 disrupts White's whole position and leaves both the g- and h- pawns vulnerable to attack. Had Black wasted even one move, White would have fortified his kingside and the old positional values would have reasserted themselves.'

That last comment echoes Spielmann's remarks about the relative values of pieces and the danger/possibility that the absolute values will come to the fore once more.

So, in general I'm very positive about this book: I really do think that everyone should be rushing out to go and buy it. There's just one thing about it that bothered me. For this edition, GM Karsten Müller has verified Spielmann's analysis with computer help and also added a few sections at the end on attacking themes and the games of Tal and Shirov. It seems very churlish to complain about something extra you are getting for free but I wasn't keen at all on the way the findings from this computer analysis were presented: in the middle of Spielmann's text in a blue typeface.

The point is: why are you reprinting this book? If you discover that half of Spielmann's analysis is incorrect and you feel that his conclusions and observations are invalidated by this, then you really need to write a new book yourself. If you decide that the mistakes are immaterial – the general observations are valid despite the mistakes – then you need to consider how worthwhile it is to point out every mistake in the text. My feeling is that the balance has gone a bit wrong in this book. I had the impression that I was listening to an interesting lecture where the speaker keeps getting interrupted by a member of the audience who keeps correcting him on irrelevant details!

For Friends & Colleagues Vol. II by Mark Dvoretsky Russell Enterprises 2015
★★★★☆

Russell Enterprises recently published *Tartakower: My Best Games of Chess* and there they left the text intact and published analytical corrections in a separate pdf that could be downloaded from their website. I felt that worked much better. The flow of Tartakower's annotations was maintained, but it was easy to check any mistakes if you felt the need.

So now on to Mark Dvoretsky's *For Friends and Colleagues Volume II*. This book is a collection of Dvoretsky's articles and interviews published on the web or in chess magazines in the past years. Some of these earlier articles have been corrected or updated with fresh material where appropriate. Unlike most of Dvoretsky's books, there are no exercises to test you, so you are allowed to read through the chess material and just gaze in wonder at the ideas without feeling guilty about not getting down to work! It's been a very enjoyable read and a wonderful reservoir of chess knowledge – I feel like I've learned tons of new positional ideas already. I found it quite interesting that the first examples that popped into my head after reading some of Spielmann's insights came from Dvoretsky's book. Masses of good stuff here, warmly recommended. The only downside is that one of my losses is in there!

Risk and Bluff in Chess is a fun book from Anish Giri's coach, the Ukrainian GM Vladimir Tukmakov. In nine evocatively titled chapters ('The Madness of the Brave', 'Masculine Desperation', 'In the Grip of Pas-

sion') Tukmakov takes us through all the facets of this mysterious dark side of chess. In all fairness, I'm not quite sure what I have learned by reading this book, but whatever that was, I had great fun doing it! As you can imagine, there's a lot of hurt and despair in the pages of this book. However, apart from the hilarious tales about Eduard Gufeld, the most shocking thing I read was undoubtedly this effort of Jobava's.

Jobava-Bok
Wijk aan Zee 2014
position after 16...♘xe4

Tukmakov presents this game in the chapter entitled 'In the Grip of Passion', which he introduces in this way: 'Do you regard yourself as a calm and rational person? If you have answered in the affirmative, with no doubt at all, then some of the decisions you will see in this chapter are likely to astonish you. Why should a player without any necessity at all, take a decision which results in the position spinning completely out of control and becoming totally unpredictable? Have you ever done this? Do you always analyse the situation from all angles and only then take your carefully-considered decision? I don't believe you! After all, if you are reading this, you are a chess player, that is a games player. And every player, no matter how experienced and calm he is, knows what it is like to find himself in the grip of almost drunken passion. That is when your actions are not guided by cold calculation and common sense but by a desperate and irresistible urge to do a certain

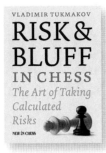

Risk & Bluff in Chess
by Vladimir Tukmakov
New In Chess
2015
★★★★☆

Learn From the Legends 3rd Edition
by Mihail Marin
Quality Chess
2015
★★★★★

Alekhine-Eliskases
Buenos Aires Olympiad 1939
position after 21… ♖xd7

thing, regardless. Usually this passion only lasts a few minutes and then you look with horror on the inevitable costs of your moments of madness. But sometimes such decisions bring success in the most surprising and unlikely ways.' Quite a build-up isn't it? Even then you are not quite ready for the following sequence Jobava decided on after just a couple of minutes' thought!

17.♖xe4 dxe4 18.♗xh6

As Tukmakov says about this game, 'The decision taken by our hero has no logic at all. Even this author, who is usually ready to explain anything, simply admits defeat.'

18…♗c5 19.♖d1 ♕c7 20.♕c1 e3 21.♗xe3 ♗xe3 22.♕xe3 ♕xc4 23.♘h5

Black's last move was apparently a big mistake after which White has a decisive attack. To be honest, I can't explain that either!

23…♕e4 24.♕g5 ♘g6 25.♔h2 ♗c8 26.f3 ♕c2 27.♖d6 ♗xg4 28.hxg4 ♔h7 29.♘xg6 fxg6 30.♘f6+ gxf6 31.♖d7+ ♔g8 32.♕xf6 1-0

An excellent book, great fun to read!

Some really wonderful books this time, but the last one is probably the best of the lot: *Learn from the Legends – Chess Champions at their best* by Mihail Marin. This is the third edition of a book which has won a number of awards, and I can't help but add my praise. Using the games of greats such as Rubinstein, Alekhine, Kortchnoi and Karpov, Marin picks out a particular facet of their skill and analyses it exhaustively. For the third edition, he had added Magnus Carlsen to the list. Some of these skills are familiar – Petrosian's exchange sacrifices and Rubinstein's rook endings – while others were a discovery for me. Tal's Super 'Rooks vs Two Minor Pieces' is an absolute joy to read, but my favourite has to be Alekhine's mastery of positions with Queen and Rook vs Queen and Rook. Marin picks out seven examples of Alekhine's mastery of such positions and does a fantastic job of picking out typical ideas and themes. I've never given such endings much thought so a chapter like this gives you a great feeling of learning something fresh! I'll just pick out one of them to show you: the queen retreat.

22.♖e8+ ♔h7 23.h4

As Marin states, 'the advance of the wing pawn not only puts the enemy king under serious pressure, but also creates the conditions for a better structure in case of further simplification.'

23…a6

Black would like to block the advance of the h-pawn to prevent White from applying pressure on his kingside. However, White has a very clever idea based on a queen retreat: 23…h5 24.♖a8 a6 25.♕e2

Attacking h5 and threatening ♕e8, invading on the back rank! All of a sudden Black is in serious danger!

Just as an aside, I checked the queen and rook endings I've played in my career. Not a bad score – 2676 rating over 41 games – but as far as I can see I've never used the backward queen move technique. So still room for improvement!

Absolutely recommended – a true 5-star book! ∎

Hans Ree

Fighting for Dignity

Robert Hübner's recent book *Elemente einer Selbstbiographie* does not provide biographical facts and only occasionally touches on chess. By writing about diverse subjects Hübner sketches the outlines of a self-portrait.

While travelling in trams and trains I like to read or re-read science fiction stories from the 1960s. This was the golden era of SF, an abbreviation that, to me, does not stand for science fiction but for speculative fiction in the spirit of Swift, Kafka and Borges. By that time the genre had long outgrown the themes that are still common subjects in films: star travel, star wars and robots.

In a 1968 collection compiled by the fine anthologist, writer and critic Judith Merrill, simply entitled *SF12*, I found a story by the English writer Brian Aldiss called *Confluence*. It is a glossary of words from the language of a superior civilization of the imaginary planet Myrin. Some of these words may be interesting to earthly chess players.

Karnad Ees The enjoyment of a day or a year by doing nothing; fasting.

OK, fine. But the next item of the glossary is:

Karndal Chess The waste of a day or a year by doing nothing; fasting.

So far, so good. I don't agree with this definition of chess, but the inhabitants of the planet Myrin are entitled

to their opinion. But then we get:

Karndol Ki Ree The waste of a life by doing nothing; a type of fasting.

What's this? The waste of a life, really? And why did planet Myrin single me out, or rather, why did Brian Aldiss?

Maybe the word being my name was just a coincidence. I am not a paranoiac who thinks that TV newscasters have a coded message especially for me. But as every Russian schoolboy and every KGB trainee used to know, harmless coincidences don't exist.

By the way, the people of Myrin had many expressions for feelings or states of mind that we earthlings find hard to describe, e.g. **Ca Pata Vatuz**, the taste of a maternal grandfather.

I showed the part of the glossary about Chess and Ree to friends. The non-chess players burst out laughing. The chess players just smiled, a bit mournfully.

Translating Finnish poetry

The Myrin attitude to chess would probably appeal to Robert Hübner, who is sceptical of everything, especially of his own achievements, which to the outside world are quite impressive.

When I saw that Hübner had authored a new book, *Elemente einer Selbstbiographie*, I ordered it immediately from Edition Marco in Berlin. This is a small company belonging to the correspondence grandmaster Arno Nickel, who also runs a good chess bookshop in Berlin.

I did not expect a book along the lines of 'My Chess Career' or 'My Life in Chess', since such self-aggrandisement would be out of character. I remember that in 1990, during one of the Interpolis tournaments in Tilburg, the journalist Herman Hofhuizen, a good friend of Hübner's, said: 'Robert has written a book. What do you think the title is?' 'Something like "My Ten Acceptable Games",' I replied. The actual title was *Fünfundfünfzig feiste Fehler, begangen und besprochen von Robert Hübner* (Fifty-five gross mistakes, committed and discussed by Robert Hübner). A later book, *Twenty-five Annotated Games*, brought the art of analysis (an expression Hübner would never use) to unfathomable complexity. I remember that at the time (1996) I played over a game from the book (Portisch-Hübner, Bugojno 1978; 21 pages of densely printed annotations), and that when I was finished, having played over all variations, I felt tired but proud, as if I had accomplished a Herculean labour myself.

Elemente einer Selbstbiographie is not a book on Hübner's chess career and it is not even a chess book, as only a few short chapters touch on chess. It provides no autobiographical facts, yet the book's title is accurate. By writing about subjects as diverse as his translation of a Finnish poem, the vagaries of modern travel and the use of 'I' and 'we' in different cultures, Hübner, in fact, sketches a self-portrait.

In his preface, which he calls a 'Fore-warning to the Reader', he writes: 'No literature is presented. No scholarship is pursued. Nothing new is said. Grop-ing, the writer tries to maintain him-self in a confusing world. He tries hard to find a stable point somewhere – but obviously without great success. Only those who harbour some curiosity about such efforts may possibly find some presentations in this book that will appeal to them.'

In many respects he reminds me of Ludwig Wittgenstein.

Squirrels and a hedonist

I found an old friend, a story called *Einhörnchen* (Squirrels) that starts with the sentence 'Unfortunately, I play chess on occasion.' It's a humor-ous piece that describes a nightmarish situation in which squirrels take over the board and both the arbiter and the opponent, and finally the narrator himself, change into squirrels. A fat dwarf says: 'Never after relishing a five-course dinner do I leave the table without having taken a digestive.' The glutton is not a favourite of Hübner's.

No wonder the narrator loses his game on time, a misfortune that I rec-ognize as a common occurrence in my own chess dreams. By the way, I may be wrong, but it seems to me that the arbiter in the story is based on the late German arbiter and tournament director Willi Fohl, who, with a thun-derous voice, used to bellow 'Silence, please!' in quiet tournament halls.

As Hübner indicates, the story had appeared earlier in *ChessBase Maga-zine* 87, April 2002, but the origi-nal version, in Dutch, had actually appeared in the Dutch literary maga-zine *SIC* in 1991. There the first sen-tence had been: 'Unfortunately I am a chess player.'

So between 1991 and 2002 Hübner, in his own eyes, had evolved from a chess player to someone who played

chess on occasion, although I would say it was more than on occasion. Obviously this corresponded with the facts. In 1991 he was still playing a Candidates' match against Timman and inevitably, having being born in 1948, he was weaker and played less in 2002. But there are many people who would call themselves a chess player till the end of their days, even if they were no longer capable of executing a move or even thinking of one.

To Hübner, not only his identity as a chess player was temporary, but the whole idea of any fixed human iden-tity appears so tenuous to him that he would say things like 'I am a chess player' or 'I am a philologist' only as a shorthand way to describe his activities, never as an expres-sion of an identity. The concept of a sta-ble 'I' is highly prob-lematical to him, and the concept of 'we' probably frightening.

He is extremely modest, often empha-sizing his ignorance and stupidity. On group photos he is always in the back rank. But he is not humble, even though he may want to be. He writes: 'Always I tend to expect malicious-ness and attempts of deception where only stupidity and incom-petence are pre-sent which surpass a degree that is imaginable to me.'

Freedom corroded

For Hübner, as for most chess play-ers, one of the greatest benefits of our profession was the personal freedom it grants. We had no masters and no servants. But freedom in chess, just as in the modern surveillance state in general, is being corroded. In the chapter '*About the arbitrariness of*

doping checks', he writes: 'The pro-tection of the private sphere is gradu-ally eroded in many ways these days. It is alarming to see how little notice is taken of this and how little resist-ance it provokes. Obviously nothing has been learned from the history of the 20th century in Germany.'

These are strong words; too strong, I think. But it's certainly true that doping checks in chess are a perverse answer to a problem that never was. Elsewhere, in other sports, they have become so pervasive that they even poison the lives of schoolchildren who do sport for fun.

Being a man of principle, Hübner gave up his place in the German national team because of the dop-ing checks. As opposed to doping, electronic cheating is a real problem in chess. But here, too, the countermeas-ures can be so brutal that a suspicion of a primitive lust for power in official-dom is warranted.

Hübner had been playing in the sec-ond league of the German Bundesliga for the Godesberger Schachklub for some time now, but recently, the entire first team of that club dissolved itself and retired from the league in pro-test against the indecent anti-cheat-ing measures imposed by the German chess federation. And it is true that they went far beyond what could be described as reasonable protection of the innocent.

I am not sure whether Hübner con-siders his retirement from the Bun-desliga a great loss to himself. He has many other intellectual interests to pursue. But it is sad for chess. ■

He writes: 'Always I tend to expect maliciousness and attempts of deception where only stupidity and incompetence are present which surpass a degree that is imaginable to me.'

Jan Timman

Never a dull moment

At the Baku World Cup a grand total of 433 games were played. **JAN TIMMAN** selected imaginative creations of local artist Shakhriyar Mamedyarov and the fierce clash between young Chinese stars Ding Liren and Wei Yi.

Knock-out tournaments with a large number of participants are characterized by an overwhelming difference in atmosphere between start and finish. In the beginning they feel like Open tournaments with big differences in Elo-level between the favourites and the lesser gods. There is a lot to see, and when following the tournament online, you have a hard job keeping track of all the games and all the twists and turns. As the tournament progresses, the number of players dwindles, as every round half of the participants have to pack their bags, and in the final rounds the playing gets emptier and emptier.

The World Cup in Baku was a slightly different story. When Mamedyarov played Karjakin in the quarter-final tiebreaks, they drew a large audience. The organizers had to add two rows of chairs to accommodate the visitors. And it's true that Mamedyarov had been growing into being the hero of the event after his elimination of Caruana, one of the big pre-tournament favourites.

KI 81.1 – E60
Shakhriyar Mamedyarov
Fabiano Caruana
Baku 2015 (4.1)

1.d4 ♘f6 2.c4 g6 3.♗g5
In his comments to Speelman-Ehlvest in 1991, Anand called this a 'strange and provocative move'. I think it's meant to be mainly an anti-Grünfeld measure. Black can still revert to the Grünfeld with 3...♗g7 4.♘c3 d5, of course, but in that case White has avoided the knight sortie to e4. The text, incidentally, had already been played in a game Model-Alatortsev in 1932.

3...♘e4 Remarkably enough, virtually all strong grandmasters react in this manner to the bishop move. Black is playing a Trompowsky with

the extra moves c2-c4 by White and ...g7-g6 by Black.
4.♗f4 c5
As in the Trompowsky. Interestingly, Black could turn it into a kind of Fajarowicz Variation with 4...e5!?, as in Rivas-Ehlvest, Logrono 1991.
5.♕c2 ♕a5+ 6.♘d2 f5

7.f3 The alternative is 7.♘f3, which is what Speelman played.
7...♘f6 8.d5 d6 9.e4 ♘a6
Not too bad in itself, but Caruana will never take his knight to b4, so it would have been wiser to complete the development of his kingside first.
10.♘e2 fxe4 11.fxe4 ♗g7 12.♘c3 0-0 13.♗e2

13...♘h5 A critical moment. Caruana must originally have intended 13...♘b4 14.♕c1 ♘g4, when

White will be forced to sacrifice an exchange with 15.0-0!. Mamedyarov would probably have liked to play the position after 15...♗d4+ 16.♔h1 ♘f2+ 17.♖xf2 ♗xf2 18.♗h6 ♖f7 19.a3 ♘a6 20.♘f3, when White certainly has enough compensation, especially in view of the bad position of the black king's bishop.

14.♗g5

14...♕d8 A strangely passive move by Caruana, which boils down to positional capitulation. There was nothing against 14...♘f4. After 15.0-0 ♘xe2+ 16.♘xe2 ♗g4 Black will have completed his development without major problems.

15.♗xh5 Of course. The black setup has been irreparably weakened.

15...gxh5 16.♘f3 h6 17.♗e3 ♗g4 18.0-0 e6 19.♕d2 ♔h7 20.♖ad1

White calmly reinforces his position. Black doesn't have a scintilla of counterplay.

20...e5 Making the situation even worse. **21.♖f2 ♘c7 22.♖df1 ♖b8 23.h3 ♗d7 24.♘e2**

Mamedyarov is going to deploy all his troops on the kingside.

24...h4 25.♔h2 b6 Another passive move. 25...b5 could have been met by 26.b4, but even in that case, Mamedyarov would probably have continued with his kingside plans.

26.g3 hxg3+ 27.♘xg3 ♖g8

28.♘h5 Decisive. The rest is the execution. **28...♘e8 29.♘xg7 ♘xg7 30.♗xh6 ♘h5 31.♘g5+ ♔g6 32.♖g1 ♕e7 33.♘f7+ ♔h7 34.♗g5 ♕e8 35.♕e2 ♘g7 36.♖f6 ♖f8 37.♖h6+ ♔g8 38.♗f6 ♖xf7 39.♕h5** Black resigned.

Mamedyarov had all kinds of fresh opening ideas. In his first classical game against Karjakin, he introduced an interesting novelty in a well-known position of the Nimzo-Indian.

NI 6.2 – E21
Shakhriyar Mamedyarov
Sergey Karjakin
Baku 2015 (5.1)

1.d4 ♘f6 2.c4 e6 3.♘c3 ♗b4 4.♘f3 b6 5.e3 ♗b7 6.♗d3 0-0 7.0-0 d5 8.cxd5 exd5 9.a3 ♗d6 10.b4 a6 11.♕b3

11...♕e7 The alternative is 11...♘bd7, which usually boils down to the same thing. In my preparations during my match against Jussupow in 1992 I concluded that the knight move is slightly more accurate.

The text has also been played quite frequently. Now White has a wide choice of plans: the automatic 12.♗b2, Petrosian's 12.♖b1, to make it possible to advance the a-pawn, and the imme-

Jan Timman

diate 12.b5, introduced by Polugaevsky. Earlier this year, Radjabov played 12.♖e1 ♘bd7 13.♖a2 against Jakovenko without achieving much. Maybe this gave Mamedyarov the idea to refine this plan.

12.♖a2!? White does not want to start anything on the queenside for the moment. He is going to take his rook to e2 in order to concentrate on the central battle. This plan entails a positional exchange sacrifice.

12...♘bd7 13.♖e2

13...b5
A strange reaction. Black fixes the position on the queenside, which means that he no longer has breaking moves with his a- and c-pawns. Karjakin had probably wanted to anticipate on White's exchange sacrifice. I think that Black's best bet was 13...♖ab8, keeping all options open.

14.♘d2
Threatening 15.f3, followed by 16.e4, depriving Black of counterplay.

14...♘e4

15.♘xd5! This is the concept.
15...♗xd5 16.♕xd5 ♘c3
17.♕c6 ♘xe2+ 18.♗xe2 ♘b6
19.e4

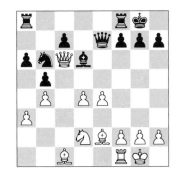

White is better. After a long and tenacious defence Karjakin managed to hold the game.

After the second classical game had finished in a quick draw Karjakin struck in the tiebreaks, to the disappointment of the numerous spectators.

Wei Yi also succumbed in the quarter-final tiebreaks. It was interesting to see how the 16-year-old star fought his way through the tournament. His style has not crystallized out yet, so his game can take any direction, switching from intensely strategic battles to tactical skirmishes. He is very well prepared theoretically.

SI 8.14 – B97
Wei Yi
Alexander Areshchenko
Baku 2015 (3.2)

1.e4 c5 2.♘f3 d6 3.d4 cxd4 4.♘xd4 ♘f6 5.♘c3 a6 6.♗g5 e6 7.f4 ♕b6 8.♕d2 ♕xb2 9.♖b1 ♕a3 10.e5 h6 11.♗h4 dxe5 12.fxe5 g5 13.exf6 gxh4 14.♗e2 ♕a5 15.0-0 ♘d7

This sharp position has been seen regularly over the last few years. Wojtaszek is the main proponent of the black system, and Areshchenko has also played it several times. The remarkable thing is that Wei Yi had played it himself with black against Yu Yangyi last year. That game finished in a draw, which is usually what happens in these kinds of hyper-sharp positions. So the position is probably in a state of dynamic equilibrium, with anything still possible. The computer cannot yet calculate very deeply. So far, White has always continued with 16.♔h1, the standard move in the Sicilian, but Wei Yi introduces something new.

16.♖bd1 This boils down to a piece sacrifice. Crucial now is 16...♕g5, which is also the main continuation

after 16.♔h1. What had he planned after this? Black needn't fear the consequences of 17.♖f4 e5 18.♘d5 ♗c5 19.♔h1 exd4 20.♘c7+ ♔f8! 21.♘xa8 ♘xf6. Maybe he had wanted to continue with 17.♕d3.

16...h3 17.g3 ♗b4
Areshchenko wants to see the proof.

18.♕e3! The point of White's play. He is going to sacrifice on e6.
18...♗xc3 Black falls for it, after which he is certain of a draw. Again, 18...♕g5 was possible. After 19.♕e4 ♗c5 20.♔h1 ♕e5 White will find it hard to avoid the queen swap, but even without the queens White will keep the initiative. He can choose between 21.♖f4 and 21.♗g4.
19.♘xe6

19...♕e5 This leads to a losing endgame. He should have accepted the second sacrifice as well. After 19...fxe6 20.♕xe6+ ♔d8 White immediately has a perpetual on e7 and d6. But he can also save it for later, e.g. 21.♕e7+ ♔c7 22.♕d6+ ♔d8 and then 23.f7 ♗g7 24.f8♕+ ♗xf8 25.♖xf8+ ♖xf8 26.♕xf8+ ♔c7 27.♕d6+ ♔d8 28.♗g4 ♕b5, and now White can safely capture on h3, when it remains

doubtful whether there is more in it than a draw.
20.♘c7+ ♔f8 21.♕xe5 ♗xe5 22.♘xa8 ♘xf6 23.♗b6
Black has insufficient compensation for the exchange. Wei Yi's technique was flawless.

Ding Liren is six years older than Wei Yi, has extensive experience at top level and has recently risen to the Top-10. In *After Magnus,* Giri has this to say about him: 'An interesting understanding of chess, combined with deep and patient calculation, makes him a very strong player'. Ding Liren is a sharp player, and his opening repertoire reflects this. The clash between the two Chinese grandmasters in Round 4 was very worthwhile.

EO 52.5 – A15
Ding Liren
Wei Yi
Baku 2015 (4.1)

1.♘f3 ♘f6 2.c4 g6 3.♘c3 d5 4.cxd5 ♘xd5 5.h4 ♗g7 6.h5 ♘c6 7.g3 ♗g4 8.h6 ♗xc3 9.dxc3 ♕d6 10.♗g2 0-0-0

11.♘g5
A novelty that he had worked out the morning before the game. Earlier this year, Wang Yue had not had much joy against Wei Yi after 11.♕a4 ♕e6.
11...♘e5
By far the best way to cover the f-pawn. Now the play gets very sharp.
12.♕a4 ♘b6
12...f6 would have been met strongly by 13.♘f7!. The white bishop pair is stronger than the knight pair.

13.♕d4 f6 14.♗f4

The fight has an unusual and fascinating character. Wei Yi thought for 30 minutes here.

14...♕xd4 The queen swap is forced. **15.cxd4**

15...♘c6!

This subtle retreat must have been the reason why Black had thought for such a long time. After 15...♖xd4

16.♗xe5 fxe5 17.♖c1 or 17.b3, Black would have been in trouble. The white knight is very strong.

16.♘f7 ♘xd4 17.♖c1

The alternative was 17.f3, after which Black will just about manage to maintain the balance with 17...♘c2+ 18.♔f2 ♘xa1 19.fxg4 e5!.

17...e5

18.♖h4!

Both players toss off the most amazing moves as if it's the most normal thing. With the text, White confronts Black with the greatest possible practical problems. The alternative was 18.♘xh8, when the following curious line is possible: 18...exf4 19.♘g6 ♘e2 20.♗h3 ♗xh3 21.♔e2 ♗g2 22.♘xf4 ♗xh1 23.♖xh1 ♘c4, with equal chances. In this case, the white h-pawn will not be particularly dangerous.

18...exf4 Afterwards, Ding Liren said that this move came as a shock, which suggests that his intuition was working well, because the text is based on a miscalculation. He had expected 18...♗xe2, which is indeed Black's best option. After 19.♘xh8 ♖xh8 20.♗e3 ♗f3 21.♗h3+ ♘f5! the position is dynamically balanced.

19.♘xd8

This fails to yield anything in the end. Indeed, White must be careful not to find himself worse. He had thought better of 19.♖xg4 in view of 19...♘xe2, which is precisely what Wei Yi had planned. Both had missed that White then has a study-like way to secure an advantage:

ANALYSIS DIAGRAM

20.♗xb7+!. This is a real hammer-blow that will please lovers of chess studies. If Black captures the bishop,

White can take the rook with check. This makes an enormous difference. White has a large advantage.

19...f3!

Now everything is fine again for Black.

20.exf3

It needed a lot of inventiveness to see that 20.♗h1! was White's best option, as it would deprive Black of all starting-points for further action in the centre and on the kingside. After 20...♖xd8 21.♖xg4 f5 White's best option is to return the exchange by taking on d4, with an equal endgame.

20...♘xf3+ 21.♗xf3

21...♖e8+!

A strong intermediate check.

22.♔d2 ♗xf3 23.♘f7

In a highly dramatic match, 16-year-old Wei Yi defeated his more experienced countryman Ding Liren to become the first Chinese to reach the last eight of the World Cup.

23...♗c6 With little time on the clock it is difficult to fathom all tactical finesses in the position. With 23...♖e2+ 24.♔d3 ♖e7 25.♘d6+ ♔d8! Black could have grabbed the advantage. The white knight has no squares in view of the check on e2.

24.b4 a6 25.a4 The position is equal, but White tries to secure the initiative with energetic play.

25...♘xa4 Incautious, because the knight has strayed too far from the scene of the battle.

26.♖e1 White fails to exploit this. Strong was 26.♖f4: Black cannot advance the f-pawn, since this would allow the white knight to land on g5 with great force. Ding Liren had overlooked that he has the hammer-blow 28.♖xg6! after 26....♘b6 27.♖xf6 ♘d5.

26...♘b6 Now the knight has made a timely return.

27.♖g4 Intending to capture on g6, but Black can defend against this. After the game Ding Liren indicated 27.♖d4 as stronger, and it's true that Black will need to defend accurately after this. After 27...♖f8 28.♖e7 ♗d5 White will have to sacrifice his knight for the h-pawn, just as later in the game. Interestingly enough, Black will be able to keep the door locked after 29.♘d6+ cxd6 30.♖xh7 by going 30...♖g8!, and White will be unable to make progress.

27...♖g8

A good defensive move here, too, but 27...♖f8 was even more accurate. After 28.♖e7 ♘d5 29.♘d6+ cxd6 30.♖xh7 ♘c7! 31.♖g7 ♘e8! 32.♖7xg6

♖h8 Black's defences will be fully organized and he will even be slightly better.

28.♖e7 ♘d5

29.♘d6+! The knight sacrifice we have grown familiar with.

29...cxd6 30.♖xh7 g5 31.♖e4

31...♖g6 Stronger was 31...♘c7, intending to keep the rook from e6. After 32.♖ee7 ♘e8 Black has built a solid defensive line that White will not be able to penetrate.

32.♖e6 Now things are getting difficult for Black.

32...g4 33.♖xd6

33...♘xb4

Black's only chance was 33...♔b8, in order to take the king to a7, mak-

ing the seventh rank less vulnerable.

34.♖h8+ ♔c7 35.♖d4 ♘d5 36.h7 ♖h6 37.♖xg4 ♘e7 38.♖g7 ♔d7 39.♖f8 Black resigns. He will have to give his rook for the h-pawn. A tremendous game.

In their second classical game Wei Yi had to try to level the score. He managed to do so in a long game with many vicissitudes.

Wei Yi-Ding Liren
Baku 2015 (4.2)
position after 64... ♖b8

An experienced grandmaster would definitely have opted for 65.♖b3, with a simple technical win. Wei Yi wants to force the position in a different way.

65.♔d5

Allowing the b-pawn to advance.

65...b3 66.d7 b2 67.♖b3

This was the plan, but now Black has a way out.

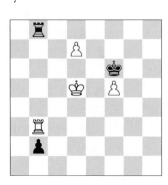

67...♖xb3! Grabbing his chance.

68.d8♕+ ♔xf5

Miraculously enough, this position is unwinnable for White, mainly because the black rook is 'hiding' behind the white king.

69.♕d7+ ♔g5 70.♕e7+ ♔g4 71.♕e4+ ♔g3 72.♕g6+

Wei Yi must have understood that the position was objectively drawn, so he gives another check in the hope that the black king will go to the wrong square.

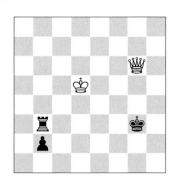

72...♔h4? And it does. Either 72...♔f3 or 72...♔f4 would have kept Black within the drawing margins.

73.♕b1

Now the black king is too far from the battleground to eventually stop the decisive queen check.

73...♔g5 74.♕c4 ♖b8 75.♕g1+ ♔f5 76.♕c5+ ♔g4 77.♕d4+ ♔f3 78.♕f6+ ♔e4 79.♕e6+ ♔f3 80.♕f5+

Black resigned. ∎

MAXIMize your Tactics Solutions

1. Bocharov-Papin
Vladivostok 2015

38.♖xe6! Black resigned in view of 38...♖xe6 39.♖f8+ ♔xf8 40.♘xe6+ ♔f7 41.♘xc7.

2. Michiels-Sumets
Ghent 2015

All the squares on the d-file are covered. Thus, White delivers a diagonal blow: **31.♕xg6!** Black resigned in view of 31...fxg6 32.♘xg6 mate.

3. J.-S. Christiansen-Tari
Lund 2015

27...♗xg3! 28.♘xg3 Also hopeless is 28.f3 ♘h4 29.♘g5 ♕f5. **28...♘f4 29.f3 ♕xg3+ 30.♔h1 ♖f5 31.♖f2 ♖h5+ 32.♖h2 ♕xf3+ 33.♔g1 ♖g5+** 0-1.

4. Ganguly-Zhang Zhong
Al-Ain 2015

39.♖d8! ♖xd8 39...fxe5 40.♖dxf8+ ♔g7 41.♖3f7+ ♔h6 42.♖h8 mate. **40.♕xf6+ ♔h7 41.♕g6+** 41.♕e7+ ♔h6 42.♖f6+ ♔xh5 43.♕h7+ ♔g4 44.♕f5+ also leads to mate. **41...♔h8 42.♕h6+ ♔g8 43.♕xg5+ 1-0**

5. Reshef-Keymer
Karpacz 2015

31.♘d7! bxc3 32.♘f8+! 32.♘xb6? c2! draws. **32...♔h8 33.♘g6+ ♔h7 34.h5!** Now 34...♘xg6 35.hxg6 mate gives no relief, while after **34...♘g8 35.♘f8+ ♔h8 36.♕g6!** Black became a victim of the Deep Fritz-Kramnik syndrome.

6. Predke-Malek
Pardubice 2015

32.♗f5! and Black is helpless against ♖b8+, with 32...♘xb6 33.♖b8+ being the main idea. Both 32...♘e5 and 32...♘e5 allow a check on b8. **32...♘e8 33.♗xd7+ ♔xd7 34.♕e5+ ♔f7 35.♕f6+** 1-0 (35...♔g8 36.♖b8+).

7. Tari-Noroozi
Urmia 2015

34.♗f5! Clearing the path to a6 for the queen. **34...♕xf5** 34...♗b5 35.♕xg4 gives White two pawns. **35.♕a6+ ♔xd5** 35...♔c7 36.d6+ ♔d8 37.♕xa5+, mating. **36.♖d1+ ♔e4?** 36...♔e5 37.♕d6+ ♔e4 38.♕xb8 f3. **37.♕e2** Mate!

8. Dragun-Bilguun
Warsaw 2015

16.♗xe4 ♘xe4 17.♘cd5 ♗xd5 18.♘xd5 ♕xc4 Other queen retreats lose a piece. Now if 19.♕xc4 ♖xc4 20.♗xe7 ♖d4 Black is on top. **19.♖ac1! ♕xd5** 19...♕xe2 20.♗xc8+ ♔d7 21.♘xb6 mate. **20.♖xc8+ ♔d7 21.♖xh8 ♗xg5 22.♕xa6** and 1-0.

9. Van Foreest-Bai Jinshi
Khanty-Mansiysk 2015

21.♖xe6! dxe6 21...♕xe5 22.♖xe7+!. **22.♗xe6+ ♔f8** 22...♔h8 23.♖xh7+!. **23.♖xh7! ♖d7 24.♖h8+ ♔e7 25.♕xg7+!** ♔xe6 25...♔d6!? 26.♕f6!!. **26.♕xg4+** 26.♖h6+ ♔d5 27.♕g4! mates in 7, but also after the text the black king can't escape: 1-0 (29).

Alina l'Ami

CURRENT RATING: 2369

DATE OF BIRTH: June 1,1985

PLACE OF BIRTH: Iasi, Romania

PLACE OF RESIDENCE: Woerden, the Netherlands

What is your favourite colour?
I like them all, but what makes a difference is the way they are combined.

What kind of food makes you happy?
Almost any kind of soup, as long as it is boiling hot! (That's why I am called 'fire woman' in my family).

And what drink?
My morning latte macchiato.

Who is your favourite author?
Mario Vargas Llosa.

What was the best book you ever read?
The War of the End of the World (Vargas Llosa)? *Don Quijote*? Too many.

What is your all-time favourite movie?
Amélie comes to mind.

What is your favourite TV series?
I liked *Breaking Bad* a lot.

Do you have a favourite actor?
I used to draw portraits of Leonardo di Caprio. As I grew up, I started to appreciate Al Pacino, De Niro, Morgan Freeman and... Bruce Willis for his witty remarks in the most terrible situations, e.g. when he was about to die.

And a favourite actress?
Meryl Streep.

What music do you like to listen to?
Rock, classical, jazz, metal, etc.

Do you have a favourite painter?
Monet, Dali, Michelangelo, etc.

What do was your best result ever?
U10 World Champion, Brazil 1995, or the European U18 title, Spain 2003. But I keep more vivid memories from winning a GM/IM tournament in Barbados in 2014 (9½/10, and me the only woman ☺).

What is your best game ever?
L'Ami-Hernandez, Carmenates, Barbera del Valles 2011. It also gave me a lot of confidence to grab a GM norm.

Who is your favourite chess player of all time?
Judit Polgar, for being a role model. Moreover, her fame didn't change her warm and kind personality!

Is there a chess book that had a profound influence on you?
I 'hated' them back then but they helped me tremendously on my way to the gold medal in the World Championship in Brazil: the Endgame Encyclopedias.

What was the most exciting chess game you ever saw?
Julio Granda Zuniga vs. Erwin l'Ami (my husband), Reykjavik 2015.

What is the best chess country in the world?
Probably Russia, but I heard Botswana is making huge progress. No kidding!

What are chess players particularly good at (except for chess)?
Getting back on their feet if destiny hits them hard, just like a tumbler toy.

Do chess players have typical shortcomings?
Complaining about trivial things. Paradoxically, they are also incredibly happy about minor details such as finding a novelty on move 25.

What is it that you appreciate most in a person?
The ability to make others feel comfortable and happy, known as emotional intelligence.

Do you have any superstitions concerning chess?
None. I like drinking my coffee before the game, which is more of a ritual than a superstition.

Who or what would you like to be if you weren't yourself?
An improved version of myself: learn more, study more, complain less and find no more excuses for my shortcomings.

Which three people would you like to invite for dinner?
MVL (sorry Maxime, it's Mario Vargas Llosa), Fischer and my late grandfather.

What is the best piece of advice you were ever given?
Margaret Mitchell through the words of Scarlett O'Hara: 'I'll think about that tomorrow... Tomorrow is another day.'

If you could change one thing in the chess world, what would it be?
Allowing a well-played game to have two winners and no loser.

What will be the nationality of the 2050 chess world champion?
If by 2050 chess is still popular, we will all be champions.

What is the best thing that was ever said about chess?
Chess will not solve your problems, but neither will water, milk, drugs or alcohol.